Cook County Education Board

Course of study of the Cook County Normal School, Cook County, Illinois

Cook County Education Board

Course of study of the Cook County Normal School, Cook County, Illinois

ISBN/EAN: 9783744792431

Printed in Europe, USA, Canada, Australia, Japan

Cover: Foto ©Paul-Georg Meister /pixelio.de

More available books at **www.hansebooks.com**

OF THE

COOK COUNTY

NORMAL SCHOOL,

COOK COUNTY, ILLINOIS.

CHICAGO:
THE J. M. W. JONES STATIONERY AND PRINTING CO.
1895.

INDEX.

	PAGE.
Board of Education	4
Faculty	5
Introduction	6
Report of Principal, 1894	15
Course of Study	44
Psychology	44
Pedagogics	46
History of Education	48
Language, Practice School	50
Reading, Practice School	53
Elocution and the Delsarte System of Expression, Professional Training Class	56
Arithmetic, Professional Training Class	56
Arithmetic, Practice School	58
Vocal Music, Professional Training Class	66
Vocal Music, Practice School	66
Geography, Professional Training Class	67
Geography, Practice School	68
Science, Professional Training Class	71
Science, Practice School	74
History and Literature, Professional Training Class	78
History and Literature, Practice School	79
Art, Professional Training Class	80
Art, Practice School	81
Manual Training, Professional Training Class	83
Manual Training, Practice School	84
Physical Training, Professional Training Class	85
Physical Training, Practice School	86
Theory and Practice of the Kindergarten, Professional Training Class	93
Kindergarten Training Class, Post-graduate	95
Outline of Work in the Kindergarten	96
Special Teachers	99
Critic Teachers, Teachers' Meetings	99
Rules and Directions for the Professional Training Class	99
Rules for Library	99
Rules for Students' Hall	100
Rules for Heating and Ventilation	100
Items of Information	101
Text Books	104

COOK COUNTY NORMAL SCHOOL.

COOK COUNTY BOARD OF EDUCATION.

Room 320, Court House, Chicago, Ill.

Regular Meetings at 11:30 A. M. on the First Saturday of each month.

	TERM EXPIRES.	P. O. ADDRESS.
HENRY F. DONOVAN, President	September, 1896	302 Webster Avenue.
ORVILLE T. BRIGHT, Secretary	Ex-Officio, Dec., 1898	320 Court House.
DANIEL D. HEALY	Ex-Officio, Dec., 1896	203 Court House.
C. S. CUTTING	September, 1895	812 Chamber of Commerce
HENRY BIROTH	September, 1895	Blue Island.
S. D. WALDEN	September, 1896	1208 Title and Trust Bldg.
NELSON A. COOL	September, 1897	Blue Island.
JOHN R. LINDGREN	September, 1897	154 Lake Street.

STANDING COMMITTEES.

TEACHERS, JANITORS AND ENGINEERS.

C. S. CUTTING, Chairman.   O. T. BRIGHT.   J. R. LINDGREN.

FINANCE AND JUDICIARY.

NELSON A. COOL, Chairman.   C. S. CUTTING.   HENRY BIROTH.

LIBRARY AND APPARATUS.

J. R. LINDGREN, Chairman.   DANIEL D. HEALY.   NELSON A. COOL.

BUILDINGS, GROUNDS AND SUPPLIES.

S. D. WALDEN, Chairman.   J. R. LINDGREN.   O. T. BRIGHT.

GYMNASIUM AND PHYSICAL CULTURE.

HENRY BIROTH, Chairman.   S. D. WALDEN.   NELSON A. COOL.

RELATION TO CITY SCHOOLS.

O. T. BRIGHT, Chairman.   HENRY BIROTH.   S. D. WALDEN.

Faculty of the Cook County Normal School.

FRANCIS W. PARKER (Principal)—Psychology, Pedagogics, Lecturer upon Structural and Physical Geography and its Relation to History.
WILLIAM M. GIFFIN (Vice-Principal)—Mathematics, History of Education, Civics and Political Economy.
WILBUR S. JACKMAN—The Natural Sciences.
EMILY J. RICE—History and Literature.
ZONIA BABER—Geography.
IDA CASSA HEFFRON—Art Studies, Painting, Modeling, Wood Carving, Illustrative Drawing and Chalk Modeling in Structural Geography.
CHARLES J. KROH—Physical Training.
ELEANOR SMITH—Vocal Music.
ANNE E. ALLEN—Principal of the Kindergarten Training Class (Postgraduate Course). Lecturer upon the Methods and Principles of the Kindergarten.
IRA B. MEYERS—Curator of Museum and Assistant Teacher of Science.
IRA M. CARLEY—Master of Sloyd.
SARAH E. GRISWOLD—Assistant Teacher of Vocal Music and Primary Methods.
MARY M. WEAVER—Librarian, Secretary and Treasurer.
LOUISE I. BARWICK—Assistant Teacher of Geography.
MRS. FLORENCE J. GARDNER—Manager of Students' Hall.

PRACTICE SCHOOL.

WILLIAM M. GIFFIN—Principal.

CRITIC TEACHERS.

ANNE E. ALLEN	Kindergarten
FLORA J. COOKE	First Grade A
GUDRUN THORNE-THOMSEN	First Grade B
MARY E. GRAY	Second Grade
GERTRUDE VAN HOESEN	Third Grade
FLORENCE M. MILLS	Fourth Grade
SAREPTA E. ROSS	Fifth Grade
SARAH E. GRISWOLD	Sixth Grade
MELVA LATHAM	Seventh Grade
KATHERINE STILWELL	Eighth Grade

INTRODUCTION.

Extract from the Biennial Report of Orville T. Bright, County Superintendent of Cook County, Ills., for the Years 1892-3 and 1893-4.

It is certainly true that the efficiency of the Cook County Normal School is greater now than at any time before in its history, and this should be the case of course. The attacks which have been made upon this school during the last three or four years, have made it more talked about and more the subject of investigation through visitation on the part of the teachers of the country, than any other school in the United States. There are now, and very likely there always will be, opinions diametrically opposed in regard to this school. But it is safe to say that among educated men and women, whether teachers or not, it gains friends every year of its existence. I believe that the friends and supporters of the school are more than doubled every year, and this because, through study of the subject, people are led to appreciate what the school stands for. During the last summer, in the columns of one of the city papers, a most virulent attack was made, or renewed I might say, by one of the members of the Cook County Board of Education, charging not only inefficiency in the conduct of the school and the training of teachers, but gross dishonesty in the administration of its affairs, especially those connected with the Students' Hall, the boarding house of the Normal School.

So far as the latter charge is concerned, I wish to say that the accounts of Students' Hall and the vouchers to prove the accounts to be correct, are and always have been open to the inspection of members of the Board of County Commissioners or of the County Board of Education. Both have been asked repeatedly to carefully inspect the accounts. Within a year and a half Mr. Charles S. Thornton and Dr. S. D. Walden spent two days comparing the books kept at Students' Hall, with vouchers, and in carefully inspecting the management of the institution. At the time, they reported to the matron in charge that they found everything in commendable order and that the books, so far as they could judge, were correct. I have personally many times inspected the books and the management of Students' Hall, and have no hesitation in pronouncing any charges as to mismanagement of that institution, during my term of office, to be absolutely untrue. The accounts and vouchers have been thoroughly examined for the months of September, October and November of this year, by a committee composed of Dr. S. D. Walden, Mr. Nelson A. Cool and Mr. Henry Biroth. They report everything connected with Students' Hall to be in very gratifying condition, and the books to be correctly kept, every item appearing in excellent form. Any statements that the principal of the school or the matron in charge has in any way benefitted pecuniarily or selfishly from the management, either of the Normal School itself or of Students' Hall, are not only untrue, but they are maliciously so. Not only this, but Col. Parker has every year spent hundreds of dollars of his own money for the benefit of the school, in the purchase of books, apparatus, and in the fitting up of the manual training room. In this respect he has been generous to a fault and it is but just that the members of the Board of County Commissioners and the people of Cook County should know the truth in this respect.

So far as the first statement is concerned, as to the inefficiency of the Cook County Normal School in the training of teachers, I wish to report as follows: In the month of February, 1894, at a regular meeting held by the Cook County Board of Education, Mr. D. R. Cameron, then a member of the Board, offered the following resolution:

"*Resolved*, That for the purpose of making a thorough test of the efficiency of the Cook County Normal School, and its value to the people of the county, the Committee upon Teachers be instructed to meet the Committee upon Education of the Board of Commissioners, and request that Committee to join with the Committee upon Teachers of the Board of Education, in the selection of a competent body of Educational Experts, who shall inspect and examine the school; and, after such inspection and examination, make a report to the Board of Commissioners and the Board of Education."

In accordance with the direction of the Board, the Secretary, accompanied by the Teachers' Committee, presented the resolution to the Board of Cook County Commissioners and asked their co-operation. They did not see fit to give it and the whole matter was laid on the table. The Cook County Board of Education then proceeded in the matter independently, and letters were addressed to several prominent educators of the United States, asking them to visit the school and report to the Board of Education their views in regard to it, as furnishing proper training for teachers. It being the last part of the school year, the Board found it difficult to secure a visit from all of those wished, but the invitation was accepted by United States Commissioner of Education, Wm. T. Harris; Dr. G. Stanley Hall, President of Clark University, Worcester, Mass.; and Superintendent Andrew S. Draper, of Cleveland, O., now President of the State University of Illinois. Under date of April 23, 1894, Superintendent Draper writes as follows:

CITY OF CLEVELAND,
OFFICE OF SUPERINTENDENT OF INSTRUCTION,
190 Euclid Avenue.
ANDREW S. DRAPER,
Superintendent.

APRIL 23d, 1894.

To the Board of Education, Cook County, Ill.

Some time since I received official notice of your action requesting me to "visit the Cook County Normal School and present a written communication to the Board as your (my) impressions of the School.

"First, as to the subject matter presented to the children in the practice school.

"Second, as to the efficiency of the teaching of the same.

"Third, as to the training of students who are preparing to teach."

For purpose of complying with your request, I visited the institution on Friday, April 13th, and spent the entire day in as close and general an examination of the work of the schools as was practicable in that time, and have the honor to submit, in the order suggested by your communication, the following statement of my impressions resulting from such examination.

First, as to the subject matter taught the children in the practice department. The course of study in the practice department of the school is well known to all who are familiar with the educational work of the country, and I found that it was being practically carried out. It is unnecessary to discuss it at length. Every line of the program is marked by a wide departure from the conventional work of the old schools. Literature, nature studies leading to the physical sciences, and manual dexterity are very much emphasized. The exact sciences are by no means ignored, but they are not held to be of first importance or essential to the discipline of the mind. The trend of the course is in the direction of real life, of intellectual versatility and general culture, rather than of mathematical niceties. Perhaps this is so to a greater extent than is advisable. That is a matter of opinion, and there will always be a wide divergence of opinions concerning it. Yet there can be no doubt about the general trend of educational opinion in the country being in accord with the general program of work in this school. Indeed, the opinion in the country has been influenced undoubtedly by the work of this school. The extent to which the work of this school accentuates the branches of work to which it is most devoted, will be found in but few other schools in the country, and it is doubtful if the general work of the country will ever go as far in that direction as this school goes. Yet the school is, in my judgment, on correct lines of work. I am confident that the branches taught the children in the practice school are well selected, well co-ordinated, and as generally advantageous to the children as any program of elementary school work of which I am advised.

Second, as to the efficiency of the teaching in the practice department. The work of the school exemplifies the course of study with apparent fidelity.

At the opening exercises each morning it is customary, after the reading of selections and remarks by the teacher in charge, to freely talk of some subject which has been announced at the beginning of the month. On the day of my visit the subject was "trees," which were budding at the time. Children of all ages arose consecutively and told things they had observed about trees, or repeated selections from literature bearing upon the subject. There was apparent freedom and spontaneity and the exercise was both interesting and profitable. The singing was full of spirit and the school showed energy and contentment.

The practice school seems to be divided into eight grades, but grades next to each other are associated in the same room. In the lowest grades at the time of my visit, the children were laying out an imaginary garden in rectangular forms. They made pictures of it on the blackboard and wrote the names of flowers and cereals which could be planted in it. Not being as full of thought upon the subject as seemed desirable, the teacher had all go to their seats and engaged them in conversation upon the subject, after which they went to the board and did better. In the next room I found the children cutting, folding and pasting paper in geometrical forms. Subsequently they engaged with the teacher in a free talk about the characteristics of the different peoples of the earth. Children of the second grade read Hiawatha and talked about the poem. They mentioned traits of Indian life and made pictures of Indian scenes on the blackboard. They moulded twigs of trees in clay. In the next room, the subject at the time of my visit was "the Sea," and the talk related to all phases of the subject. The children told what they knew and attempted, very successfully, to make pictures of light-houses, etc., on the board. The teacher drew their knowledge from them, supplemented it with her own, and guided and directed and stimulated their minds. They looked up articles relating to the sea to read, and read them off-hand with considerable feeling and expression. There were live fishes in the room, which lent added interest to the subject. In the next room the subject was "water-sheds," and it was treated in a similar way. While I was in this room, relaxation was afforded through physical movements at the word of command of one of the little girls. The exercise was well performed. In the next room the subject was "the soil." The constituent elements and the proportions of each were discussed. Quantities were here involved and arithmetical computations resulted. This was undoubtedly true in other ways in other rooms, but this was the first in which I observed it. In this room the children were writing with ink and doing very well. In a room of the 5th and 6th grades, the subject at the time of my visit was "the atmosphere," and the treatment was of the same character as in the grades below, except that it became more elaborate with increased years of the pupils. This will suffice for all the grades of the practice department.

The topics discussed were related to real life and had much interest for the pupils. Geography was necessarily and continually involved. The correct use of language received incidental but frequent and sharp attention. The thing most aimed at was fullness of thought and freedom of expression in the belief that incidental matters would necessarily follow, and the thing aimed at seemed to be secured in unusual measure.

I observed the kindergarten work, the different phases of manual training and an exercise of the entire school in physical culture, in which the teachers, pupil-teachers and pupils occupied alternate positions, and which was conducted by the general teacher of physical culture, with much satisfaction.

The moral and social tone of the school seemed to be excellent. There was very little of the conventional in the way of organization and discipline. Children seemed free from any unnecessary restraint. They communicated with each other and occasionally moved about without asking permission, yet they seemed disposed to do right, and ready to conform cheerfully to the necessary requirements of school life. When there was some confusion, a word from the teacher was sufficient to arrest it. They were manifestly on pleasant relations with their teachers. The extent and almost entire uniformity of interest in the work which was manifested by the pupils are gratifying. Teachers and pupils seemed to work together for a common end, in which all were interested. Spontaneity and originality were encouraged, and there was much physical and intellectual life in the school, yet it seemed to be controlled and directed, so far as was necessary, through appeals to the nobler impulses and emotions, and without much show of force.

Through some periods of the day, the practice schools were in charge of the training-teachers of the Normal School faculty, and at others in charge of pupil-teachers, under the observation of the training-teachers. It is impracticable and unnecessary to say much here about the question as to whether the frequent changes of teachers which is thus necessarily involved, is advantageous or otherwise to the children in the practice schools. That depends upon the quality of the work in the Normal School proper. If the requirements for admission to the Normal are sufficiently exacting, if the faculty is strong, if the supervision is close, there are unquestionably certain advantages to be derived from the system over the work which is likely to be done by the average teacher in the ordinary school.

In my opinion, the members of the faculty of your Normal School are generally, and in many instances unusually, competent and devoted to their work, the public-teachers' average of higher grade, and have had more experience than is generally the case in the normal schools of the country, the supervision seems to be close and critical, and the teaching in the practice department is performed with a marked degree of efficiency.

Third, as to the training of the students who are preparing to teach. The members of the Normal School faculty were evidently persons of culture and possessed of a large measure of pedagogical training. They were of middle life or below it, apparently very enthusiastic in their work, and thorough believers in the theories of the school. The students in the Normal department seemed, in general, more mature than is usual in such schools. A considerable number of young men and women who had probably never taught, were present, but it was quite clear that many persons of experience as teachers had dropped their work and gone to the school for special preparation. Upon inquiry, I was told that such was the fact, and also that many had come from long distances for that purpose. All the work of the student seemed to be marked by a good degree of intelligence and a very unusual degree of earnestness. I was present through the recitation of one of the Principal's classes in psychology and also at the general meeting of the Normal students, at the noon hour when the children in the practice-schools had gone to lunch, for the consideration of the morning's experiences in the practice-schools, or of any pedagogical question which might be presented by any member, which meeting was also conducted by Col. Parker. Both of these exercises were full of interest. The class in psychology showed that some of members at least were doing strong and deep thinking. All manifested great interest in the discussion. The pedagogical class was a free-for-all experience meeting marked by much life, and generally enjoyed.

I have no doubt of the efficiency of the Normal department of the institution. This much I am able to say as the result of general impressions. If disposed to particularize at all in this connection, I should say that the strong points of this department are the completeness with which the habit of original inquiry, of going to the bottom of things, is aroused, and the extent to which love for and enthusiasm in a teacher's work is intensified. These points are surely secured to an unusual degree, and they are the leading elements in a teacher's equipment.

CONCLUSION.

I would not have it supposed that I have attempted to cover, in this statement, all of the work of this school. I have simply endeavored to state facts which were presented to my mind, and thoughts which were aroused by a day's visit. It was not possible for me to see all of the work of the school, but what I saw was not selected for me, and I have no doubt it is typical of all of the work of the institution. If so, then the whole institution is characterized by good cheer, warmth, freedom, energy and earnestness. It is operating on sound pedagogical principles, as I understand them. If there is any criticism to be placed upon its work, it relates back to the preparation of the course of study. The course of study as formulated, is admirably carried out in my judgment. If the circumstances were different, it might be advisable to give the exact sciences more prominence, relatively, in the course of study. But, taking into account the unusual characteristics of the students in the Normal department, and the apparent circumstances of the pupils in the practice schools, I am far from sure that even that would be advisable.

An educational institution is about what the principal makes it. The Cook County Normal School is the exemplification of the views and theories of the distinguished principal. Under his management it has gained celebrity in the country. No one is expected to believe all that he believes. Not all would be able to go so far as he goes in his particular lines of work. Probably it is not desirable that they should attempt to do so. But the fact remains, and it will hardly be called in question by any one at all familiar with the educational work of the country, that he has broken out roads along which the multitude is following. His conceptions of good school-work, of what ought to be taught, of methods of managing pupils, of securing their interested attention and arousing their self-activity, have exerted a decided influence upon and given a decided impetus to, the educational work of the country, for which he will ever be gratefully remembered. To do all this it has been necessary to be very earnest and intense. I am confident that his special views concerning a course of study and the intensity with which he carries them out, are of no disadvantage to the pupils in the practice department which is not more than compensated in other ways. And I am sure that those views and that earnestness are of decided advantage to the students who are in training for teachers, and to the general educational work of America. I am, gentlemen,

Very sincerely yours,

(Signed) ANDREW S. DRAPER.

Under date of May 21st, 1894, Dr. G. Stanley Hall writes as follows:

THE AMERICAN JOURNAL OF PSYCHOLOGY.
EDITOR'S OFFICE.
Clark University, Worcester, Mass., May 21, 1894.

My Dear Mr. Bright:

I spent the entire day, Friday, May 18th, 1894, in Col. Parker's school and with him and his teachers, as I have done before. We visited nearly, if not quite every room, and I came away with a large bundle of papers, pamphlets and books, showing the work of both instructors and pupils, which I have been diligently reading since. Of course, I ought, as I should like so much to do, were I not tied to my own work, to spend a week or two there in the study of details, but one who is used to visiting schools can catch the main features in a rapid way from even a brief visit.

I come away with a yet higher impression of the value and the soundness of this work. The improvement since my visit of two years ago is most marked in the upper primary grades, where perhaps it was most needed. The points that strike me are the harmony of work and spirit among the instructors; the co-operative feeling which permits no waste in jangles; and the great efficiency of all, and especially three or four of the instructors which I wish it were not invidious to name.

Best of all is the great conception that nature and man are the two chief objects of study, and that the intrinsic interests that center about these should subordinate reading, writing, and parts of arithmetic. Such subordination of form to substance as is now really carried out there is exactly the opposite of the two prevalent tendencies to bring form and pedantic details to the front, and let substance drift into the background. The admirable treatment of myth to warm the heart toward nature; the copious use of natural objects and the garden; the amazing readiness of the children to write, draw, and even sing alone, without self-consciousness; the general unity of subjects which allow concentration full scope; and the sympathetic insight into child-life,—all these features make a most striking ensemble, and as beneficent as it is striking. The amazing influence that this school, as a whole, and its principal and teachers individually have had on lower grades of instruction in this country, has been surprisingly wide as well as deep. To weaken that influence now when it seems just attaining the full, but—as everything good in education must be—slow maturity of its usefulness, would be a national calamity.

I have read with care the criticisms and examination papers in criticism of the school, and have received various publications attacking it. I think they must impress an impartial mind as due not so much to the natural criticisms of extreme conservatism or to personal spite as to some entirely extraneous, alien, and perhaps material interest. I know nothing of the matter whatever, but think I feel as the astronomers who find perturbations not entirely accounted for by any known or obvious cause.

I have one or two minor criticisms. First, I think physiology entirely condemns the extreme side attitude while the tip of the seat and the incessant writing make it all the worse. My second criticism is rather a desideratum and may have a personal element. I think if Col. Parker would look into the results of the new psychology and of the technical methods of child study he would find unexpected resources of strength in his own directions, and also more effective modes of expressing his own admirable ideas.

I am, very truly yours, G. STANLEY HALL.

And under date of September 1st, 1894, U. S. Commissioner Wm. T. Harris responds as follows:

DAPARTMENT OF THE INTERIOR,
BUREAU OF EDUCATION.

WASHINGTON, D. C., Sept. 1, 1894.

Col. F. W. Parker, Cook County Normal School, Englewood, Ill.:

MY DEAR COL. PARKER—I have tried in vain since my visit in Chicago last March to write up my notes regarding your school as I promised. A host of things important to do have been of necessity laid aside for lack of strength to do them. But to-day I received from you a copy of the Chicago *Evening Post*, dated August 29th, and addressed in your handwriting. I turn at once to the article which speaks of the new members of the County Board of Education and of the proposition to make a change in the principalship of the Cook County Normal School. In my opinion your career in that school has been a very noteworthy one. I think that you have done a great work for the cause of education. Your influence has tended towards the invention of devices which interest children in their studies, and in the work of the school, and thereby decrease the amount of external pressure hitherto found necessary to secure work from these pupils. Such instrumentalities as the rod, the harsh word, the browbeating demeanor of the teacher necessary to secure earnestness on the part of the pupil, have given place to this new idea of education, the idea of interesting the pupil himself. This new idea dates from Pestalozzi. But I think that you deserve a high place in the list of pedagogical reformers. Your book, "Talks on Teaching," contains, in my opinion, more helpful ideas for interesting the pupil in his studies and helping him to clear ideas than any other book of pedagogy ever published.

You know, of course, that I have always disagreed with you in regard to many things—matters of detail and matters of theory. But I think that any Normal School that secures you for principal has a great piece of good fortune, and I think that the County Board of Cook County will appreciate this very good fortune and retain you as long as you are willing to stay. I think that a man so eminent as you are, and so efficient in pushing new methods that are unquestionably reforms on the old methods, should be retained in position and your salary increased, notwithstanding there are many things in your theory and in your practice which are not approved by others. All strong men keep their positions because of their strength in some great lines of policy. All strong men have points which others disapprove. Happy is the Normal School that has a great educational leader like yourself at the head of it. I saw very many highly meritorious features in your model school when I visited it last March. Nine-tenths of the work was highly admirable according to my standpoint.

You are at liberty to show this letter to any person or persons, or to publish the same in case it is desirable. Of course I do not suppose for a moment that the County Board of Cook County wish to consider my name for a place in your Normal School, and it is therefore impertinent for me to say that I do not seek a place in any Normal School, and would not accept any place were it offered me.

I shall write you soon concerning your new book, "Talks on Pedagogics," which has come to my book table.

Very sincerely yours,

[Signed.] W. T. HARRIS, *Commissioner.*

The moderation of these three communications, I think, will strike every fair-minded reader, and nobody can be left in doubt as to the confidence felt in the work done by Col. Parker in the Cook County Normal School, as a means for the education of teachers.

When a case is on trial, there are two things which have to be considered—First, the evidence given; second, the credibility of the witnesses. The case is the Cook County Normal School. The plaintiff in this case is Charles S. Thornton, a Chicago attorney, with no experience whatever in school work. The three witnesses quoted above in the defense of the school and of the work of Col. Parker, are all engaged in active educational work now, and have been from fifteen to forty years each. Their reputation is as high as that of any three men in the United States, and it is not confined to the United States by any means. Dr. Harris was, for many years, in charge of a grammar school in St. Louis; for many years following he was superintendent of the St. Louis schools, and for the last six years he has been United States Commissioner of Education. His position places him at the head of the public schools of the United States, and his great ability, learning and experience eminently qualify him for the position. Dr. G. Stanley Hall has attained a reputation in the field of "Child Study" second to that of no living man. He is president of the important university of technology at Worcester, Mass., and was formerly a professor in Harvard University. President Andrew S. Draper was an eminent attorney who became state superintendent of the State of New York, which position he filled with distinguished success. He afterwards became superintendent of the city schools of Cleveland, administering them with marked ability, and this fall he has been inaugurated as President of the University of the State of Illinois. He has already given that institution a vigor and life which it has never known before. These are the witnesses, gentlemen. You may draw your own conclusions from their evidence. And to their testimony might be added that of scores of other eminent educational men in the United States, whose opinions of the Cook County Normal School are formed from personal observation.

SIXTH BIENNIAL REPORT

OF THE

Cook County Normal School.

Gentlemen of the Cook County Board of Education:

In compliance with your request, I have the honor to submit my Sixth Biennial Report of the Cook County Normal School.

In former reports I have endeavored to present to you the general plan of the school, the Course of Study, and all that pertains to its external movements; in the present instance I shall attempt a description of the inner work of the school, and some of the more important results which have been the outgrowth of a plan steadfastly adhered to through twelve years.

Normal Schools were established upon the belief that there is a Science of Education, and, consequently, an Art of Teaching. This Science of Education, like all other sciences, except mathematics, is still in process of development, and in common with the majority of the natural sciences, has been well nigh revolutionized within a few years. A new psychology has been evolved from the old psychology; premises upon which almost universally accepted methods were founded, have been swept away, and more rational and sensible ones have taken their places. A broader psychology emphasizes the fact that the whole boy goes to school, brain, heart, and muscle; that all are needed by each one; that neither can be educated separately.

The common school system of the United States, the system that proposes to educate every child in the Nation at public expense, is, comparatively, in its infancy. Great purposes bring great thoughts, and it is safe to affirm that after fifty years' experience in the establishment and promotion of the common school, the thought of many intelligent people and of all educated and trained teachers is turned to the problem of the Science and Art of Education. The Science and Art of Education are limited only by the possibilities of human growth. In a democratic scheme of government, it is plain to see why our teachers in the past have not comprehended that there is, or should be, a Science of Education; for the growth of our common system of schools is directly dependent upon the intelligence of the average citizen. Primary and secondary education has been further hampered by the fact that until within recent years, American universities and colleges have not practically acknowledged the Art of Teaching; indeed, even now, it has not fully come to its own, but occupies a somewhat debatable place in the majority of college and university curriculums. The more progressive have recognized this fundamental truth by the establishment of Chairs of Pedagogics. All honor to the University of Chicago that has thus early in its history founded a Department of Education under the leadership of Dr. John Dewey!

The common school was born of the people; it is the purest democratic growth of any institution extant. The pedantry of the past has infected the people, and the result is that the greatest obstacle to progress in education is the indifference they manifest in regard to the possibilities of work in the school room. This is shown clearly by recent discussions of methods and means of education; discussions from which the opinions of all the educators and experts of this country and Europe were carefully excluded. The average lawyer or business man would retire in disgust if asked to join in consultation over a severe case of diphtheria, and diphtheria is always with us! We may even have had it ourselves and *survived it*.

The Cook County Normal School was established in 1868, and has had a severe struggle for existence. It is not alone in this. All Normal Schools have had to make their way with exceeding slowness into the hearts of the people. Weighted with the ignorance, presumption, conceit and pedantry of the past; with few helping hands reaching down from scholastic heights; bowed beneath the burden of material progress in this great Metropolis of Chicago, education is, at present, far in the rear, as witnessed by the prevailing idea of what children should be taught in the schools and of what education really is.

Prof. D. S. Wentworth, my honored predecessor, gave his valuable life to the founding and maintenance of a Normal School in Cook County. He had to overcome distrust, apathy and indifference. Commercial institutions bring to the people direct financial results; that which fosters the higher spiritual growth needs weights and measures more delicate than those which determine the value of gold or silver, and education is the Cinderella of progress. As a rule, the best comes last.

Democratic growth has its horrors, and among them, as a principal factor, is found the low estimate of educational means, and the delusion that subjects of study need only to be *legislated* into the schools in order to become a part of the life of children. From this delusion has sprung much of recent discussion. The only means on earth by which educational subjects can become of educational value to our children, and form an essential factor in character building, is through the educated, trained, sympathetic, devoted teacher. Tested by the same system of merit by which all other practical matters and businesses in this world are governed, three-fourths, at least, of the teaching force of this country would be eliminated from the schools. Our schools, for the greater part, are in the hands of inexpert, untrained, uneducated teachers; the blame for which state of affairs does not rest upon the teachers, but upon the people who employ them. The introduction of new studies, subjects that have been foisted upon them during the last few years, has resulted simply in overburdening the teachers and mystifying the pupils. As a rule, the fewer studies an inexpert teacher has, the better. The "Three R's," with a smattering of geography and a sprinkling of history, are quite sufficient for an untrained novice, or a teacher whom experience does not teach.

The fundamental problem towards which the educational thought of America is now gravitating is one which other countries,—notably Germany and France—have already solved; *it is the problem of the educated and trained teacher.* The reason why movement in this direction has been slow is evident. The selection and election of teachers in large cities is almost entirely without any Civil Service method. True merit is not demanded, and therefore it is not forthcoming. Our schools have been made, under existing political systems, an asylum and a refuge for the uneducated and the untrained. The argument for trained teachers is incontrovertible: the practice is the antipodes of the argument. The people spend millions for schools; but it is a matter of general indifference whether the return for money expended shall be one per cent. or a thousand. Here at least the "Almighty Dollar" does not enter into the count. We have a very costly system of supervision, but that system of supervision consists principally in suppression; instead of granting the liberty whereby teachers may become free, they are "cabined, cribbed, confined." There is a goodly per cent. of teachers, who, if they were given the proper help under expert supervision, and left unhampered by formal examinations and unreasonable limitations, would more than treble their efficiency.

Mr. Wentworth received his inspiration from the movement in Massachusetts under the leadership of Horace Mann. Like Horace Mann, he saw that there could be little or no progress in the common schools without training schools, and used all his influence for the establishment of the Cook County Normal School. He had to overcome the apathy of the people in regard to the imperative necessity for artist teachers; the situation was further complicated by political and business agencies which had to do with the establishment of the school in Englewood, agencies which are still active to the detriment of the best interests of the school.

THE EDUCATIONAL MOVEMENT IN THE SCHOOL FROM JAN. 1, 1883.

One movement probably stands above all others, and that is the introduction of the study of the elementary sciences into the school, and the training of teachers to carry this work into primary and grammar grades. Parents and citizens have had an opportunity, of late, to study opinions only upon one side of this great question. It may be well to give them the authorities in favor of the study of the elementary sciences, or, as it is at present called under Mr. Jackman's able leadership, "Nature Study." It will not be necessary to give all the authorities or to trace the growth of this movement from the beginning. Pestalozzi, the best known of educational reformers, in his struggle to overcome the terrible inertia resulting from the teaching of dead forms, went straight to nature as the best means of stimulating children's minds. He was not the first, but among the first, who used systematically natural objects in the teaching of all subjects. In a degree he understood what Shakespere meant by "Sermons in stones, books in running brooks, and good in everything." His motto was, "Education is the generation of power," and he sought for the source of that power in the manifestations of eternal wisdom in nature. The work of Pestalozzi permeated the schools of Germany, and is now making its way slowly in all the schools of the world. Nature study has been the corner-stone of primary education in Germany for more than fifty years, fulfilling the prophesy of Fichte, who said, "I await the regeneration of Germany from the methods of Pestalozzi." Froebel, in the very name of "Kindergarten," emphasizes in the strongest way the value of nature as the fundamental means of education. Rousseau, before the time of Pestalozzi, had strongly urged the teaching of nature, especially the true teaching of geography. Paul Bert, the eminent statesman and scientist, promoted the teaching of the elementary sciences in all the schools of France; his text-books upon elementary science are well known in America. The pedagogical literature of England is filled with directions for object teaching or science study. Every scientist with humane tendencies, from Bacon down, has urged the teaching of the sciences in the schools. Huxley, Spencer and Helmholtz have, in their pedagogical works, advocated the fundamental principles of teaching science in the primary schools, and presented methods for such teaching.

There is not a Normal School in the world which does not endorse the teaching of science. In America, the Oswego Normal School is the pioneer in this direction. In short, *it can be said without the slightest fear of contradiction, that every eminent educator of to-day, in all civilized countries, believes firmly in nature study from the kindergarten to the university.*

If science study could have been introduced under its true colors, there would have been no opposition on the part of the people. But the science teaching of the past had left a residium of disgust that was hard to overcome. Notwithstanding the universal and decided concensus of opinion on the part of all educational authorities in favor of the introduction of elementary sciences into primary and grammar schools, it has been met by the usual opposition on the part of those who have not taken the pains to investigate. Indeed, the opposition has been nearly as strong to this innovation as it was to Webster's Blue Back Spelling Book in 1787. Humanity is not always ready to receive the good which is offered it, and much of opposition is negative rather than positive. A community holds only here and there a mind in which the seed of new truth germinates. The accepted truth of to-day is ever the despised and rejected truth of yesterday. Honest conservatism has all unwittingly worked hand in hand with veniality to blind people to the fact that science study in reality means the *enhancement of common sense*, the simple putting of reason into the common every-day work of the world.

It will be readily granted, that in the schools of the past, that which touches us closest, the earth we walk on, the air we breathe, the water we drink, the clothes we wear, all that exerts potent influence upon life and general well-being, sanitation, hygiene, cooking, comfort and progress, had little or no place. Science study means bringing the children in closer contact with their environment; it means putting common sense into their actions; it means that the housewife shall put a little chemistry into the very important art of cooking; it means that heads of homes shall understand sanitation, hygiene and that which pertains to health and comfort in the home, that which shall make it a more wholesome place in which to live and rear children; it means the better health and comfort of the community at large and the banishment of many superstitions that have led to plague, sickness and death. Surely these things are of practical value, and by no means detrimental to the bread and butter side of the question so strenuously insisted upon as the end and aim of primary education. It means that the farmer shall know more of the products of the soil and the soil itself, and how to apply a little chemistry in this direction also; that he shall know more of the nature of trees and plants, of insects which destroy crops and those which protect them. It means that the boy who goes into manufacturing shall have a trained insight into the work of machinery, shall grasp and adapt himself readily to new and varying conditions. It means an intense interest and appreciation of ever-changing phenomena; it means a cultivated taste and a power of adjustment to environment. It means that children shall come in touch with the spirit of the age in which they live, and into true communion with God as manifested in His universe.

Discoveries in science, made by a score of men, have revolutionized the civilized world of to-day. The child is living in this great current of progress, and it stands to reason that he should move with it, understand it, feel it, know it, be at one with it. History indicates the direction of human progress; science provides the way. Science brings to the door of the school-room the most fruitful and richest products of the world's experience. Its introduction means that the common schools and the common people shall have the best that the world affords; that knowledge of science shall not be confined to the few who work their way through the university, but that all children shall have an appreciative knowledge of and a great love for the study of nature and its marvelous works. These are the practical reasons why children should study nature. If through this study home can be made happy and health preserved; if through it the vote of each citizen shall have some intrinsic value when he puts it into the ballot box to decide questions of sewage, drainage and all that pertains to the life and growth of a community, then it is in the highest degree commendable and not to be banished at the nod of asinine authority.

Another thing education in common schools should accomplish —it should point to and prepare the individual for the vocation to which he is best adapted; for the more all-sided the growth, the better the chance of making one's way in the world. A few trades and professions are now greatly overcrowded, while the world waits for competent engineers, skillful farmers, expert mechanics and trained manufacturers.

RELATION OF SCIENCE TO READING AND WRITING.

The arguments in favor of nature study by well known authorities would fill a volume, but there is one, and of unquestionable practical value, which every intelligent person must recognize. Pestalozzi found that through nature study, the common branches, i. e., the "Three R's," could be more thoroughly and quickly taught than through the old grind of isolated and disconnected letters, words, facts, and definitions. The great obstacle to progress in the schools has been mere formal study without the impulse of intrinsic thought. It is the universal testimony that wherever nature studies have been introduced, *the children learn to read, write and cipher with greater ease, and greater accuracy.* If nature studies had no other value than this, it is reason enough for their maintenance.

It is asserted that children leave school in great numbers at the end of the third year, and therefore have not time for anything but the so-called rudiments, the tools without which the best which life has to offer cannot be attained; but it can with greater force be argued, and with truth, that the reason children leave school is because they dislike the school. This dislike is well founded. They must have that which enters immediately into their lives and which they can assimilate. You cannot make the human mind fall in love with dead formal study. What of the thousands of children who would stay through the grammar grades, high school, and enter the universities, if the work in the lower grades were more reasonable? Isn't it about time that the child's nature and needs enter as a factor into the discussion? It is borne out by all experience that when children have a living impulse of investigation, experiment and research in the realm of nature, the reading, writing and arithmetic come in as a matter of course, a matter of necessity, and the outworking is far more profitable than when the teaching is confined to the acquisition of dead forms and empty symbols. Insistance upon this mind disintegrating drudgery stultifies the soul of the child, drives him from school at a most dangerous age, and imperils his whole future.

But it must be constantly borne in mind that the foisting upon the schools of studies, no matter how strong the argument is concerning their intrinsic value, has been, and always will be, a failure, without the educated, trained, and competent teacher. It is only in comparatively recent times that our teachers have had an opportunity to really study science. The nominal study of science, natural philosophy, chemistry, and the like, in our high schools, brought little knowledge and still less love for these sciences. Therefore, many untrained and partially educated teachers look upon these subjects with such repugnance that it is extremely difficult for them to understand their real merits. Teachers of dead forms have their ruts already made, their routine established, and they do not wish to turn out of their fixed tracks for other and untried ways. The introduction of new and valuable material that is to bring beauty and truth to the child, means wakefulness and alertness where have been unperplexed repose. A superficial skimming of these subjects will not suffice. Trained supervisors who understand the subjects to be taught can do much to arouse in the minds of teachers a great sympathy and belief in nature study and consequent skill in teaching, but it is up-hill work; the large majority of our teachers have little or no education in science, and little or no desire to learn. The pre-eminent value of any one subject of study is one thing, the teaching of that subject is quite another. I submit this brief discussion in order to show clearly that before science studies can be used as potent means of education, the trained teacher is an imperative necessity.

Convinced of the feasibility of this broadening of the curriculum of primary education, at the beginning of my administration, under your direction, I sought for a teacher who was working along these lines: It is needless to say that to find competent teachers at the present time in this direction is an exceedingly difficult thing. Prof. H. H. Straight was elected—a teacher in the famous Oswego Normal School, and a pupil of Agassiz, who probably did more than any other one man for the introduction of nature study into the schools of America. Prof.

Straight was assisted by his accomplished wife, who was also trained in the knowledge and methods of science. No explanation is necessary to you who are so well acquainted with the difficulties and obstructions in the way, when I say that our movement in the direction of natural science at first was slow indeed. It was a field of experiment. A Normal School should not have for its aim, alone, the preparation of teachers to do the work already done in schools, but should be, as J. M. Greenwood, Superintendent of Schools in Kansas City, wisely says, "an educational experimental station," a pioneer in new and better work. The first attempts were tentatively successful, but still they were not in the highest degree satisfactory. There was a failure to relate practically the science studies with the other studies, although Prof. Straight held the ideal of concentration firmly in theory. After the death of Prof. Straight, his wife took up the work, and carried it on successfully to the time of her resignation to accept a position in the Imperial Normal School at Tokio, Japan.

Your Board, in spite of partial failure, still held an unalterable belief in the value of nature study, and intrusted me with the difficult task of finding the man to formulate a system and methods in this direction. Then followed some experiments in teachers which were not entirely successful. It does not necessarily follow that a man who has studied several years in a university can therefore teach science.

You were successful in electing Wilbur S. Jackman, a graduate of Harvard, and a teacher in the Central High School of Pittsburgh. Mr. Jackman applied himself heart and soul to the study of the situation. It was agreed that children guided by instinct and acting spontaneously, acquire an elementary knowledge of all the sciences. The main thing to be done was to bring children face to face with nature in the school, by means of a properly arranged course of study. A complete reformation of the ordinary school curriculum was of first necesssity; the attempt to exhaust any one subject, or to carry the children beyond their power of inference, is pedagogically wrong.

RESULTS OF NATURE STUDY.

The outcome of Nature Studies in this school up to the present time may be stated as follows. The subjects have aroused a great enthusiasm and love for study: the children do not cease their study at the doors of the school room, but come into a warm contact with nature; the weather, clouds, vegetation, animal life, all appeal to them in a natural, wholesome and educative way. It is found that the place of all places to study nature is out of doors, in the field, surrounded in a large way by the objects and movements of nature. Our experience but repeats that of Germany fifty years ago. We have proved past question that the most profitable elementary study of geography and geology, as well as the other natural sciences, is outside the school room.

Second, the organic relations between science study and the "Three R's," tested by long experience, have been established. This study arouses in closely related sequences a body of intensely interesting thought. This thought is thoroughly organized and compacted by reading, writing and the art modes of expression. Under the white heat of thought words and sentences are written upon the board. Under the impulse of intrinsic thought they are easily grasped and retained. The retention is enhanced by immediate action on the part of the child, who writes because he has direct need for that form of expression. By this procedure, which springs from the present necessities of the child, reading and writing, spelling and grammar, become indispensable incidents to thought evolution. The economy of this process is apparent to every rational being. The many phases of the one subject presented by a teacher who understands her profession, afford the necessary amount of drill, and the bugbear of the primaries is banished. Genuine work takes the place of unscientific drudgery. Common sense is applied in the study of arithmetic. Numbering is measuring—measuring forms in space, or measuring matter; there can be no study of science without the continual application of numbers; under this application the child feels the necessity for, and gains the needed knowledge and skill in arithmetic.

No small outcome of the science study has been its application in art. The development of mental images which lie at the foundation of all mental growth, is enhanced by art studies. Modeling, painting and drawing are applied to the development of thought. It was found that art should be taken from its isolation and put into real life and action, should yield itself to the evident demand for its peculiar forms of thought expression; the countless opportunities afforded by the study of science for the expression of thought with clay, pencil and paint brush are utilized. The fundamental means for developing the giant sense, that of touch, is clay modeling. The famous "mud pie" is the head of the corner in education, and will find its true place; it is a part of the eternal fitness of things and cannot be banished.

To sum up our experiences in science. *First:* There is developed in the child an intense love for science, and a thoughtful contact with his environment. *Second:* Continual original experiment becomes a habit with the child. *Third:* Reading, writing, spelling and grammar are taught more thoroughly and economically than under the generally accepted dead form teaching. This is perhaps the most satisfactory outcome, for it is proof of the value of nature study that cannot be honestly disputed. *Fourth:* The teaching of elementary science, in an all round way, is made the foundation of all other teaching. It gives the children plenty of interesting and educative work; it absorbs their minds in their work, and otherwise wasted energy is thus utilized; the tendency towards disorder and mischief-making in our children is avoided, through absorption in genuine educative mental and physical movement.

GEOGRAPHY.

One of the principal nature studies is geography. Humboldt, Ritter, Guyot, Richthofen, and others, have revolutionized this subject, to whose discoveries and methods, when added the researches along the line of geographical geology of our own scientists, Drs. Chamberlin and Salisbury of the University of Chicago, teachers have at their disposal an immense amount of valuable and usable material. The Science of Geography has been practically re-created. The foundation of all geographical study is the study of the surface forms of the earth. This study brings the child into direct contact with the surface of the earth, with the history of that surface, and with the drainage of the earth; this implies geology, and indirectly, meteorology. Indeed, in the new geography is concentered all the other sciences. Political geography which forms the stock of most of the present and past teaching of geography is relegated to history, where it properly belongs. History is closely allied to structural geography.

That which is true in other nature studies also applies in the highest sense to geography: the teaching of reading, writing and arithmetic is closely allied to the teaching of geography; geography develops in a broad and high sense the imagination, which is constantly enhanced by reading, by writing, and by art studies. Here again the mud pie is made a potent influence. The children model the earth's surface. The simplest art work children can do is to tell in sand what they observe of the earth's surface in their field excursions. The movement in geography has kept pace with the other movements. The work is now directed by Miss Zonia Baber, one of the most thoughtful students in this direction in America, one who has given a great deal of careful study to geology and to the new researches in geography.

At this day and generation, it is an absolute necessity that the American citizen know something of the whole earth, and of the relation of the whole earth to his own country. The earth has become very much smaller through the marvelous inventions of the age; railway, telegraph, steamship and telephone, make the earth one neighborhood. Primary education must adapt itself to changing and growing conditions and thus it will be seen that the study of the distribution of heat, air, moisture, vegetation, animal life, and man's life, is the culmination of all primary nature study.

HISTORY AND LITERATURE.

Closely allied to nature study, is history and literature. This work was the earliest organized in the Cook County Normal School. Miss Emily J. Rice, one of the graduates of the famous Oswego Normal School, is at the head of this department, and has been connected with the school for twenty years. The pupils are taught history from the beginning, throughout the eight grades. The earth is the home of man. Its climate, moisture, vegetation and animal life have had from the beginning, and always will have a powerful influence on the development of the human race. The teaching of history is the teaching of the struggle of man towards civilization and higher development; thus, history cannot be taught to children through the mere teaching of United States history. Our government is the outcome of all the past, is the culmination of progress in the direction of human freedom, and children cannot understand what they have cost without understanding the long succession of heroic efforts of the people who have lived and died for them. History is intimately related to geography and to all nature studies; it is founded upon myth, which is the embryo of all human growth; it is the child spirit of the world which appeals powerfully to the child, and is the foundation of his after spiritual unfolding. Miss Rice arouses great enthusiasm in this department. The outcome of the work done in history can be briefly stated. The children study the history of human liberty in the direction of freedom from the first. History is closely corelated or united to all the other studies.

The great function of literature is to throw headlights upon human progress. The fundamental or central studies of science, geography and history, including literature, furnish the children with an inexhaustible source for mental and moral activity. They furnish conditions which give the children, from first to last, plenty of educative work. They are really three great branches of one subject—human life and the laws of its environment. History and literature should cultivate a correct taste, foster a strong love, and form habits and methods of reading and studying the best and purest literature. Children properly taught will continue to read good books, simply because the best appeals to them, and because their taste is developed above that which is trashy or vicious.

EXPRESSION INDISPENSABLE TO THE DEMAND OF THOUGHT POWER.

As I have already said, within the past twenty-five years the science of psychology has been practically revolutionized. The researches and investigations of eminent scientists in the direction of physiological psychology have been brought to bear on the study of rational psychology, and both have converged into a strong movement in the direction of child study. It is too early in the investigation to look for a body of doctrine, but there is a general concensus of opinion already in regard to the relation of expression to thought development. Briefly stated, the evolution of educative thought is absolutely dependent upon expression, or, expression is the indispensable means for intellectual growth.

This utter dependence of educative mental action upon thought expression demonstrates the organic relation between the mental and the ethical. Mental action is weak and inoperative until it is functioned; expression which is not "thoroughly informed" with thought, cannot properly perform its function of reaction. Thought and expression are organically related in the functioning or manifestation of thought through the body, which thought enters into the life of the pupil, and becomes a part of himself.

The theory of the organic relation between thought and expression has been looked upon as fundamental in the work of the Cook County Normal School. It may be said that the first systematic attempt to relate all the modes of expression into one organic whole, and to relate expression to thought as a means of enhancing it, was begun in this school. It has had its rise in the teachings of Delsarte, who was one of the first exponents of the reactive influence of bodily acts and expressions upon the mind. From this standpoint, investigations in the direction of expression and its reactive influence, moved on, and all the different modes of expression, gesture, voice, music, making, modeling, painting, drawing, speech and writing, were used to itensify, concenter and expand thought, upon the hypothesis that each mode has its individual function, and that the results of each are organically related.

It will be readily seen that in the teaching of science, geography, history, arithmetic and geometry, the art modes of expression, modeling, painting and drawing, become an absolute necessity. These modes are practically indispensable to the strengthening and enhancement of the powers of observation. When a demand is made for modeling, painting or drawing an object, the attention is closely, carefully and systematically directed to that object. No other means will bring about such careful and close observation. This is one of the greatest offices of art, the stimulus to observe.

All expression must be genuine, must be a genuine reflex of the image aroused and united by observation. Any proper attempt at expression of an image enhances the growth of that image. Second, the products of observation are carried over to the action of the imagination. It will be readily granted that the foundation of all education consists in the educative use of the imagination; imagination is not only functioned but intensely stimulated by the reactive influence of the attempt to externalize the image. The commonly accepted theory of the organic relation of thought to expression is in striking contrast to the prevailing practice in the school room, in which art is thrown outside, or is entirely isolated from the subjects of study, where pupils are required to draw flat copies, which have no relation whatever to any educative subject. Persistent and steadfast efforts have been made on the part of the faculty to relate all exercises in expression organically to thought itself. This has been going on steadily for twelve years with varying success, but with success enough to thoroughly convince us that there can be no such thing as an all round education without the constant use of each and every mode of expression. Much remains to be done; but a strong, earnest and faithful attempt has been made to exercise the whole body in thought manifestation so that there will be the greatest and strongest reaction upon the development of the mind.

Art expression, as I have said, must be genuine with little children, that is, the genuine reflex of the individual image; and when such reflexes are in themselves crude, it simply indicates a correspondence to an imperfect image. All art attempts of children are the reflexes of crude images and must be in themselves crude and imperfect, if there be educative reaction upon the growing image.

The outcome of the method applied is that the children have a great love for art; it soon becomes an indispensable medium of manifesting thought; they instinctively express themselves in clay, with the brush and pencil. Inclination is enhanced by exercises which demand only what a child can do through a proper action of his mind and will. Taste in art is cultivated when the demands for art are genuine. The drawing of flat copies, the construction of simple conventional forms, according to the best authorities in psychology stultifies and kills art feeling. There can be no better test of the growth of the mind than through the genuine expression of the child in the different art modes of expression. No one will deny that in all the varying functions of life, in whatever place or position the pupil may find himself in his active duties as a mechanic or professional man, in fact, in all directions, power to express thought by any one or all the art modes of expression, is of immense importance; under proper direction it is also possible that every pupil in our public schools may acquire this skill.

Your Board will understand the amount of research and study required aside from the mere direction and teaching of this subject, in such a practically untried field. Miss Ida Cassa Heffron has struggled earnestly and faithfully with the problem. Owing to the deficiency last year, your Board was obliged to dispense with the services of Miss Helen Gregory, who was a valuable co-worker with Miss Heffron. The efficiency of the work of this department has been greatly crippled by lack of teaching force.

MANUAL TRAINING.

Within a few years, perhaps fifteen at the most, manual training has been actively discussed by educational circles. At first, it was strongly opposed, but gradually the opposition lessened until now it is practically accepted as one of the branches in our common schools. Twelve years ago, a manual training department was established in the Cook County Normal School under the direction of Geo. F. Fitz, now a professor of Physiology and Hygiene in Harvard University. It goes without saying that there was very little sympathy with this movement at first. Again, as with art, it was the first systematic attempt in this country to make manual training a regular branch of study in all primary and grammar grades. The celebrated Sloyd method of manual training was not then generally known. Suffice it to say that a room in the basement of the Cook County Normal School was crudely fitted up with a few tools, paid for by the generous bounty of the citizens of Chicago. Charles H. Ham, who did so much for the Twelfth Street Manual Training School in Chicago, was of great assistance in this direction. Manual training has continued as a part of the curriculum of the school ever since.

Five years ago Walter J. Kenyon, a graduate of the Cook County Normal School, took the course at the celebrated Sloyd School in Naas, Sweden, and introduced the system of Sloyd now in our school. All the children of the practice school and all the members of the professional training class have had this course. Much remains, yet, to be done in this direction, but a few results may be stated. First, all pupils, without exception, have great fondness for manual training. It seems, as in art studies, that the mind naturally gravitates towards making things, a desire to put thought into substantial realities. Second, the children of the school become skillful in doing all kinds of manual work. The school furnished the children for the sloyd in the Children's Building at the World's Fair. This sloyd department was under the direction of the most prominent teacher of Sloyd in the United States—Gustaf Larsson, of the Rice Training School, Boston, Mass. Mr. Larsson was unstinted in his praise of the activity, willingness and skilfulness of the children who worked under him. In this connection, it may be said that the school also furnished the children who worked in the clay modeling classes in the Children's Building, under the direction of Mrs. Holland of Concord, Mass., a teacher from Mrs. Quincy Shaw's famous school in Boston. The University of Illinois proposed to make a large Geological Relief Map of Illinois, seventeen and a half feet ($17\frac{1}{2}$ ft.) long. Two firms took the contract to make the map, but gave it up owing to failure to secure workers skillful enough to perform the task. As a last resort, the projectors of this plan applied to the

Cook County Normal School. The school furnished Miss Louise Barwick, a graduate of the training class, and several other pupils, some of whom were of the Eighth Grade, and the work was successfully accomplished.

Not long ago, the surfaces of the desks in one of the primary rooms needed repairs. The pupils of the Eighth Grade were requested to do the work, which they entered into heartily, scraping off all the old varnish, and polishing the desks. The work was done in a perfectly satisfactory manner; trained artisans could not have done it better. It is the testimony of all that the children of the school earnestly engage in any work which requires thought, skill or energy, and carry the work to a successful end.

Third, manual training furnishes one of the best possible means of physical training. Pupils suffering from nervousness in the practice school and the training class, have overcome their nervousness to a great degree by taking this course. Fourth, the manual training work has been closely related to all the other work, especially in physics, where simple apparatus is continually needed. This work has been done by the pupils in the sloyd room satisfactorily and efficiently. Fifth, manual training furnishes the best possible exercises in drawing, elementary logic, arithmetic, and form study. Manual training properly taught lays a strong and sure foundation for both arithmetic and geometry. Sixth, sloyd work is of the first practical value in life work. The civilized world is filled with incapables, who have never done any work systematically, and therefore are incapable of entering successfully upon any work in life whatever. Manual training is the systematic development of purpose, not only does it engender a love for work, but what is equally valuable, a habit of doing work thoroughly.

ARITHMETIC.

Probably no innovation has been more marked, and appeals more to the common sense of thoughtful people, than the innovation in the direction of arithmetic. Numbering, say the psychologists, is measuring. In the prevailing arithmetic, figures are generally used in an abstract way, with but slight appreciation of their real function. The pupils are not made to *feel* the necessity of arithmetic. Through the teaching of science and geography, arithmetic was made an absolute necessity, that is, everything studied had to be measured and related, and problems for numbering both in history and geography, were of constant occurrence.

A child learns the facts of number by applying the facts to genuine study. A child feels the necessity of number when he uses the number for its highest possible value to him and to others. The application of arithmetic to all subjects goes steadily on and the results are sufficient to show that the tendency is a right one. It is endorsed by the highest psychology, and, indeed, by good common sense. We learn to do by doing; we learn arithmetic by using that arithmetic and applying it to central purposes. The question may be asked: How much of drill is still necessary for tables, and otherwise? The answer is near at hand. Drill may be with or without thought, or, in other words, numbers may be functioned for their legitimate purpose in learning them, or they may be learned apart. The rule is, the more thought there is back of a numerical fact the more effective the drill, and the less the necessity for drill without thought. Under Dr. Giffin's able direction, arithmetic is becoming a more and more prominent factor in all instruction, and is tending steadily towards a successful issue.

PHYSICAL TRAINING.

The body, and the whole body, is the organ of the mind. The mind has a vital relation to the body, and depends upon it for its best action. The body is an organ of sense action, or an organ of reception of thought, of attention in its three modes, observation, hearing-language and reading; it is also an organ of motor discharge or expression. These are simply statements of an old doctrine that not only received a great impulse in all Greek education, but had a renaissance through the efforts of Father Jahn and other great believers in physical training.

Many, if not most failures in life may be laid to lack of vitality, lack of physical power. Thousands of pupils, by overstraining in one direction, become the victims of nervous prostration, and drag out a miserable existence as chronic invalids, or come to an early death. Constant sitting and bending over badly made desks, holding the eyes with unchangeable focus upon text-books, result in weakness and deformity of the whole body. Without physical training, many muscles of the body are practically unused. The result is congestion or atrophy of nerves and nerve centers, the fruitful cause of countless diseases.

Four years ago, your Board elected Mr. Karl J. Kroh as teacher of physical training in the Cook County Normal School. The physical training had been pursued for previous years in a desultory way. Mr. Kroh is an eminent representative of the Turners, and in addition to this, he is an earnest, indefatigable worker in this field. He is a great lover of children, observes them closely, and is most successful in the adaptation of his work to individual pupils. Mr. Kroh trains the teachers of the practice school, who, in turn, train their pupils. He also prepares the members of the professional training class to do the work of physical training in whatsoever schools they may find positions. It would be impossible in a few lines to state the results of Mr. Kroh's work in the school. It is sufficient to say that it has been marked for good in every direction. First, by the enthusiasm with which pupils enter into physical exercises; and secondly, by the enhancement of the mental work through systematic training. The Cook County Normal Practice School takes a large number of defective pupils, pupils who are too nervous to go to other schools, pupils defective in sight and hearing, pupils who have suffered under the derangement of the motor centers. Mr. Kroh, and indeed, all the teachers, give special attention to these particular cases. Third, modern psychology tells us that the development of the will depends largely upon the development of the muscles, and it has been found in our school that many pupils who have been called bad because they had not the power of self control, have been greatly assisted by physical training. Fourth, the whole tone and government of the school is far better through Mr. Kroh's indefatigable efforts in training the body as an instrument of the mind.

One needed addition could be made to the school, and that is a department of physiological psychology. The teacher in this direction should be a trained physician, who could give advice in regard to the general physical condition of the pupils. There are many pupils in school who are there to their own detriment, and should be at home or out in the fields at play, rather than struggling to overcome the impossible. A child, for instance, who has had scarlet fever, is not capable of doing mental work for one or two years thereafter, and any attempt to do such work only leads to mental depression.

KINDERGARTEN.

The essential work of a Normal School should be to embrace all the advance movements in education. Probably no one factor in education during the last quarter of a century has been so potent in the advancement of teaching and training children, as the kindergarten. The all-controlling idea of Froebel, the founder of the kindergarten, was a recognition of the dignity of childhood; of the immense value of instinctive and spontaneous activity. Froebel's doctrine met the old doctrine of sin and depravity inherent in the child, face to face. The tendency of all civilization, with the exception of the Greek, was to sink the individual into the mass, into the government, into the controlling idea of church and state. The new doctrine that was strongly foreshadowed by Greek education, found its highest outcome in the doctrine of Froebel, in the reconciliation of the individual with the state, under the altruistic idea. No movement in our times has had a more widespread influence upon American education, than this doctrine of Froebel's. Its pioneers began their work when there was little or no movement in any direction in education in the United States, but more especially in the East.

Mrs. Alice H. Putnam, pioneer of the kindergarten work in Chicago, under the auspices and support of the Froebel Kindergarten Association, took charge of the kindergarten work in the Cook County Normal School, twelve years ago. For a time, the training class of the kindergarten was removed to the Normal School, and Mrs. Putnam not only taught the training class, but took charge of the kindergarten, as well. She did this as she has done much other work, without, at first, any salary, and somewhat later at a very meager one. The Cook County Normal School has had the kindergarten as an essential factor in the school work for twelve years. Little children are taken at four years of age, and kept under the training for two years, when they enter the lowest primary grade.

No thoughtful believer in Froebel's doctrine will claim for a moment that Froebel's exposition of his own methods, forms the end of all real kindergarten work. Froebel expounded a great, all-embracing doctrine of education, and under the very force of circumstances presented a method which he believed would and should be constantly developed higher and higher as circumstances permitted. The influence of the kindergarten has permeated the whole school; it is the practical beginning of the doctrine of concentration. Its fundamental idea is the social idea; little children come together and learn to help each other in play and work. This social factor is a tremendous factor in all education. Its underlying idea of mutual assistance, "everything to help and nothing to hinder," has been carried throughout the whole school.

MUSIC.

It is perhaps needless to discuss the immense educational value of music. The Cook County Normal School has been greatly favored by the services of two eminent teachers in this direction. First, Miss Lizzie Nash, one of the most skillful of Prof. Wm. L. Tomlins' teachers, under whose direction music was ably taught for several years. She aroused great enthusiasm in this direction, and a strong love for music. Her work is still felt in the school. She was followed by Miss Eleanor Smith, who has spent several years in Germany, and is herself a composer of note. Under Miss Smith music has been brought to bear upon all the other studies; the music is selected with a view to this purpose. Miss Smith's talent in composition comes in play, as children's music, from the educational standpoint, is not always to be found. Each critic teacher is personally trained to use music as a means of reinforcing the work of the school room, and in the morning exercises, music takes a more and more prominent part.

DEPARTMENTAL INSTRUCTION.

One motive has guided the faculty of the Cook County Normal School in all its efforts, and that is to train its pupils in the professional training class to be skillful in all directions of school work; in other words, to avoid the necessity of departmental instruction by special teachers. It is not in place here to discuss departmental teaching. It may be sufficient to say that it is utterly opposed to the fundamental doctrine of concentration. The regular teacher of a class or room should be able to present all the subjects taught and use them in the best possible way as means of education or character building. Every teacher, for instance, should be able to give the pupils the proper physical training. In the first place, teachers should be physically trained themselves, should understand the theory of such training, and should know how and when to use it. A special teacher comes at set times during the week, which times may or may not be adapted to the best good of the children. The teacher of a room should be able at any time, when there is inertia on the part of the pupils, when there is a flagging of attention, to change the work, not only by giving the pupils physical exercise, but by giving them music. Art can only be properly taught by the regular teacher, who understands the relation of the art to be done to the subjects taught. This is true in all directions. A vast amount of money is now paid for special teachers, which might be turned, with great profit, into salaries which would command the services of the best teachers.

CONCENTRATION.

The tendency of all the work of the Cook County Normal School has been in the direction of the corelation and unification of studies. In the above presentation, this direction has been indicated. Concentration is now the great central problem of education in the United States and elsewhere. The first attempt, and the most prominent attempt to put this doctrine into active practice, I think, was in the Cook County Normal School. It was a slow and gradual development. Its foundation, as I have already said, came from the doctrine of Delsarte, and was applied to reading, writing, and the art studies. A resumé of the practical value of concentration may be made.

I. The first and last steps in reading may be best taught under the impulse of intrinsic thought gained through the studies of science, geography and history. Reading is taught as an incident to the evolution of thought; under this method that which has appeared before as a great obstruction to mental action, —for instance, the learning of letters, phonics and forms of words—has been overcome. When the child needs to know a form, and that is when he wants to use it, he will get it with the greatest ease. The reading, instead of being desultory, isolated from subjects, is turned directly upon the subjects. Nothing is read but literature, which is made an effective means for the study of science, geography and history. This proposition appeals to common sense. One does not need to be versed in the science of pedagogics to comprehend it. Formerly reading was taught by itself and the emphasis placed upon purely mechanical preparation; this is dispensed with, the mechanics of reading can be exercised and learned under the mental energy generated in consciousness, an energy that comes with interest and earnest study.

II. Writing, which has been taught formerly as an isolated subject, has been gradually and practically brought under the doctrine of concentration; all the forms of writing, from first to last, are learned as speech is learned. Indeed, the mechanics of speech is far more difficult than writing. We have found that children can learn to write, and include all the forms of spelling, sentences, and grammar, by using writing freely as a means of thought expression. No one can enter the school and closely study it without seeing that this has been accomplished. In other words, to sum up the advantages of the doctrine of concentration in reading, writing and spelling, as now applied, it takes no appreciable time to teach reading and writing, because they are made essential means of thinking.

III. All the art work, modeling, painting, and drawing, are made means to an end, rather than ends in themselves. The great influences of art work have been brought to bear upon thought itself. Prof. James, the celebrated psychologist says that man is a reactive animal, and art will be taught in a most effective way when reaction upon thought is appreciated and utilized.

IV. Arithmetic and form are used in all the subjects taught. We have not yet reached that point of excellence whereby we can say that there is no special drill by itself; but without question, as we move on in research and practice, formal arithmetic will be taught, and taught thoroughly, through its application to all the fundamental studies.

V. The children have a sufficient number of educative subjects for their highest mental action. Children have been lost mentally, and even morally, because of the lack of right conditions. Misdirected energy has led to vice and crime. It is the purpose of concentration to conserve energy, and by utilizing it, bring about the highest development of the body, mind and soul. The fundamental law of pedagogics is that all educative growth is by self-effort and self-activity. Children are naturally active. The necessities of these activities are met, and in the best possible way, through the application of the theory of concentration.

QUALITY VS. QUANTITY.

The old idea of education, and the present prevailing one, is the idea of quantity, pedantry—so much actual spatial work must be done, so many pages studied, so many lessons learned, and so many books gone through, so much gone over and finished, so much marking to register quantity alone. For this millions of dollars are spent and time and toil wasted, both on the part of teachers and pupils. Under the idea of concentration, the ideal is quality not quantity, process not product, culture not acquirement. It stands to reason that in the accumulation of studies in the school, or the so-called "enrichment of the course of study," if quantity is still made the end and aim of the teachers, they stand helpless before the demand. If we take in the elementary sciences, art studies, music and physical training, and in the five or six hours of the day try to accomplish a definite something in the way of quantity, the case is utterly hopeless. Herein lies the difficulty. While the quantity ideal holds, there can be no real enrichment of the course. Under its domination, the less the number of studies the better. The "Three R's" are quite sufficient for its meager demands. Under the ideal of quality, however, the whole earth, all the richness of past learning, all the investigation of the present time, all of individual experiment and research, are called into full play for the development of character.

We hear a great deal of complaint, and justly, in regard to the great number of children who leave school at the end of three years. There is a serious mistake in regard to the reason why these children leave school. They do not leave school because they are poor, for there are thousands of fathers and mothers who would work their fingers to the bone in order to keep their children in school, if their children really liked school, really wanted to learn; parents would do their utmost to help children if they had any special desire to be helped. Children leave school because they dislike school. They would rather be in the street, in the factory—anywhere, but in school. And the reason is not because they have not sympathetic teachers, not because they have not the closest supervision; it is because they have not the conditions for all-round, harmonious work; their active lives are not met with something that they feel is right and good to do. It is found that children in manual training schools, like the Chicago Jewish Training School, remain because they love the work, and parents are willing to have them stay. The old ideal of quantity crushes out the life of the children. There are, of course, some boys and girls who make their way; there are geniuses who overcome difficulties and become strong in spite of methods. There are others who become pedants and accumulate a great mass of facts, and find eventually a market for their wares. But that upon which all educators in all time have agreed, but few teachers have acted upon, is the center of quality, or character; the formation of genuine habits of thought and action; the love of study and habit of study; these are far above the mere acquisition of knowledge. It may be said here that most of the prevailing methods in schools are methods of inheritance. They come down to us from the time when tyranny, or the rule of the few, obtained; when the individual was little thought of, sunk into the mass, a mere tool to carry out some theory of government; degraded by the selfishness of rulers. The theory which trains American citizens must be compatible with American genius, must be the working out of the highest good of the individual for the whole, not into the whole. It is this theory of education which the doctrine of concentration would foster.

There is another opinion that is doing great harm, and that is that the common school is for the *common people*, and that poor children should have a peculiar education suited to the condition in which God has pleased to place them. The real democratic principle is that poor children should have the best education which it is possible for brain to devise or heart to conceive. That education which does not train a child to work, to love work, and to put his brains into work, is worthless. That education which does not develop the highest aesthetic appreciation of the true, the beautiful, and the good in art and literature, is worthless. That education which does not bring the child face to face with the underlying principle of our government, each for all and all for each, and lay the foundations of good citizenship, has failed of its purpose. That education which does not convince that the law of the Lord is perfect, enlightening and quickening the spirit, does not carry the seeds of future possibilities to the nations.

SCHOOL GOVERNMENT.

When I came to the Cook County Normal School, twelve years ago, I held a strong belief that children could and would govern themselves, if they had the right conditions for self-government. I believed that the sole function of education consisted in the presentation of the right conditions for self-government. I had been for many years under the domination of the old methods; I had believed with all my heart in will-power, in the dominance of the teacher; had, through fear, bribery, marks, or personal influence, controlled my pupils. Following the example of countless other teachers, I had imposed my will upon the child, and held his personal will in abeyance. But a closer study of true democracy, and a more intimate contact with children, gradually changed my opinion. I began to see that little citizens, under a tyrannical government for twelve or more years, could not thereafter truly exercise the sacred function of free citizens. All the hopes of mankind depend utterly upon self-government, upon the realization of true democracy. Strong in this belief, I came to the Cook County Normal School to apply this theory and prove its validity. It is needless here to recount the failures to you, who have so carefully and sympathetically watched the progress of the school. It was difficult to find teachers who believed in self-government on the part of the children; that children could govern themselves ever so much better than older people; that a great love could be developed in children for others; that they had this love; that it was innate; and that by presenting the right conditions, it could be strongly cultivated; who understood that pupils must have full conditions for educative self-activity in order to realize this free development of personal will-power. The courage to be crude!

>"It was never for the mean;
>It requireth courage stout.
>Souls above doubt,
>Valor unbending,
>It will reward,—
>They shall return
>More than they were,
>And ever ascending."

All corporal punishment was put aside, and the usual substitutes for corporal punishment—bribery, marking, giving of rewards—infinitely worse than flogging as a means of school government, were not employed. Of course, the difficulty was to find the right conditions by which children could use their whole minds and bodies in the direction of self-development. We had repeated failures, especially in the first few years of my administration; failures which largely had their root in the unbelief of the teachers themselves. There was a lack of faith in childhood; the old idea that children were full of innate depravity and prone to evil dominated them, in spite of themselves. To put the new ideas into practice, "Ah, there was the rub!" Indeed, the principal himself had a great struggle to find means to this one end. But the children were made to feel, in time, that the least of a teacher's duties is that of police, or watching for errors in action, misbehaviors. The responsibility of work was put upon them and they were trusted to do their work and to do it well. In short, we appealed to the best in them, and they amply repaid our trust. A school should be an ideal democracy in the fullest sense of that word; until our common schools are founded firmly upon this ideal, our republican institutions are constantly endangered. One cannot be governed tyrannically until twenty-one years of age, and then become a self-acting, self-determined member of the body politic. It is impossible.

THE WORK OF THE PROFESSIONAL TRAINING CLASS.

I have presented the work of the practice school because the practice school is the essential means by which the pupils in the training class are inducted into the science and art of teaching. Theory has but little effect until it is put into the concrete, into the lives of the children. The most potent influence over the training class is the work of the practice school. First, faith in better methods is developed and strengthened by the work which they see done. Second, all the work of the professional training school concenters upon the practice work.

I have given, in former reports, an exposition of the general plan of this practice. I can say that it becomes better and better as the work goes on, mainly through the indefatigable study and persistence of the critic teachers. Every bit of work done by the professional training class is thoroughly prepared under the direction of the special and critic teachers; their teaching is carefully observed, and every possible means taken to eliminate all poor work, so that that which is presented is good and helpful for the children. The members of the professional training class come in contact with all grades of the school from the lowest primary to the highest grammar, throughout the course of the year.

The fundamental studies of the professional training class are—first, psychology; second, pedagogics, and third, history of education. This latter subject has not been treated as it should be. There should be a teacher of the history of education. It is now in the hands of the principal and vice-principal, who have not time to work it out satisfactorily.

Each teacher of a special subject, or head of department, has charge of that subject. It is his or her work to see that pupil teachers have the necessary knowledge to present the subject, and, second, to have a knowledge of the method of presentation, so that each head of department is not only teacher of subject matter, but also teacher of the psychology, principles and methods of that subject. The head of each department is also supervisor of the work done in his or her subjects.

Graduates of High Schools, four years' course, are received into the Professional Training Class for one year's training. An extended description of the results of twelve years' training in primary, grammar and high school, as we find them in our pupils as they enter the school, might be profitable and suggestive. It is sufficient, however, to say here that very few have the necessary knowledge to begin the work of learning how to teach. The reason why so much more text-book work is done in the common schools is because teachers are not masters of their subjects. The great weakness of teaching is not fundamentally a lack of knowledge in methods, but a lack of knowledge in subjects. Knowledge obtained simply from text-books, memorized verbatim, never reaches anything like an extended knowledge or love for that subject. Experience proves that it takes one year for the ordinary high school graduate to get fairly started in the work of learning how to teach and to become aware of the knowledge imperatively needed for educative teaching. A second year, in our experience, is absolutely necessary to develop that which will insure efficiency as a teacher. Graduates of colleges, on the other hand, and teachers of long experience, can take the course in one year. The whole idea of the school is to surround the members of the training class with the best possible influences, which influences shall lead them to appreciate the possibilities and responsibilities of a teacher's life. It is not possible even in one or two years for a student to get the knowledge he will need in teaching or to fully understand the principles and methods to best apply that knowledge; but if a sense of limitation is felt, and if a great ideal of the art of teaching is aroused, then the student who graduates from the school and enters into active practice of teaching will continue a life long student.

It is very gratifying to the faculty of the Cook County Normal School to know that the work they have successfully pioneered in the past has been appreciated by their co-workers of the educational world, all over the United States.

Allow me to say one word in regard to the faculty of the Cook County Normal School. You have selected them with the greatest care, and there is hardly, at present, a member of the faculty who has not a strong influence upon educational matters in every part of the country. Most of them have written books upon education; many of them appear at meetings and institutes of teachers, and are quoted as authorities upon special subjects. They are one and all assiduous, earnest, honest students of education, who apply what they believe to be true, and work together unselfishly for the interest of the children and members of the training class.

Allow me again to thank you heartily on behalf of the faculty and myself for the generous and cordial support you have always given the school. Respectfully,

FRANCIS W. PARKER.

COURSE OF STUDY

OF

Professional Training Class

AND

PRACTICE SCHOOL.

PSYCHOLOGY.

Professional Training Class.

FIRST TERM.

The purpose of the study of Psychology in the Professional Training Class is to acquire a knowledge of the laws of mental activities, their growth and development, in order to understand and apply the science of education.

Psychology is the study of the conscious activities; the greatest difficulty in this study is to separate in thought, conscious action from the external causes of such action.

I. PRODUCTS OF SENSE-PERCEPTION.
 a—Psychological definitions of "I see," "I hear," "I touch," "I taste," "I smell." *b*—External causes of conscious action. *c*—Examination of external energies. *d*—What is an object? *e*—What is the conscious effect of an object acting upon the mind? *f*—Correspondence of external cause and conscious effect. *g*—What is an external attribute? *h*—What is an elementary idea? *i*—What are their relations to each other?

II. SPECIAL STUDY OF PHYSIOLOGICAL PSYCHOLOGY, under Mr. Jackman.
 a—Dissection of the brain. *b*—Examination of the sensorium. *c*—Study of sense organs.

III. GENESIS OF ELEMENTARY IDEAS. *a*—Sensation. *b*—Perception.

IV. INDIVIDUAL CONCEPTS, EXTERNAL CAUSES.
 a—Objects, pictures, models. *b*—Oral language. *c*—Written and printed language. *d*—Symbols—pure and partial.
 MENTAL CAUSES. *a*—Fancy. *b*—Imagination.

V. PRESENTATION, REPRESENTATION; the difference in the mental acts. Are they different?

VI. ASSOCIATION OF ELEMENTARY IDEAS.
 a—Recollection. *b*—Remembrance. *c*—Synthesis. *d*—Compared. In what do these acts differ? What is analysis? Relation of analysis to synthesis.

Second Term.

VII. CLASSIFICATION. *a*—Spontaneous classification. *b*—Scientific classification. *c*—Relation of language to classification.

VIII. JUDGMENT AND INFERENCE.
a—Limitation of sense products. *b*—Scope of judgment and reason.

IX. REASON, LOGIC.
a—Relation to the power of judging. *b*—Instinct. *c*—Intuition. *d*—Spontaneity.

X. THE WILL.
a—What are the beginnings of will power? Is every conscious act of the mind an act of the will?

XI. MEMORY.
a—Association. *c*—Remembrance. *d*—Automatic mental action. *e*—Scientific basis of memory.

XII. THE EMOTIONS.
a—Feelings. *b*—Emotions the effects of thought. *c*—Relation of emotions to desire. *d*—Effect of emotions upon the agents of expression.

XIII. MOTIVE.
a—Utilitarian. *b*—Altruistic.

XIV. PSYCHOLOGY OF ATTENTION.
a—Observation defined. *b*—Hearing language. *c*—Elements and construction of oral language. *d*—Idioms. *e*—Phonics. *f*—Emphasis. *g*—Reading defined—reading and hearing language compared. What is a written or printed word? What is its use? How is it learned? Relation of a word to a sentence.

XV. PSYCHOLOGY OF LANGUAGE.
a—Spoken. *b*—Written or printed.

XVI. PSYCHOLOGY OF THE MODES OF EXPRESSION.
a—Gesture and voice. *b*—Music. *c*—Making. *d*—Modeling. *e*—Painting. *f*—Drawing. *g*—Speaking. *h*—Writing. *i*—Mental and physiological effects of learning forms of expression for form's sake.

Third Term.

XVII. PSYCHOLOGY OF FORM AND GEOMETRY.
a—Relation to knowledge and mental development. *b*—Practical use, the relation of form to geometry.

XVIII. PSYCHOLOGY OF NUMBER AND ARITHMETIC.
a—Number defined. *b*—Use of number in reasoning. *c*—Practical use of number. *d*—Operations in number.

XIX. PSYCHOLOGY OF
a—(1) Geography, (2) Science, (3) History. *b*—The unity of studies.

XX. PSYCHOLOGY OF THE THEORY OF CONCENTRATION.
a—Unity of a state of consciousness. *b*—Unity of an act of expression, unity of the body. *c*—Unity of the being. *d*—Economy of effort. *e*—Unity of thought and expression. *f*—Unity of knowledge. *g*—Unity of laws. *h*—Intensity of mental action. *i*—What subjects of thought induce the most intense mental power? *j*—Relation of attention, (observation, hearing language and reading), to subjects of thought. *k*—Relation of form and number to subjects of thought. *l*—Relation of modes of expression to subjects of thought. *m*—Relation of physical training to brain power—"A sound mind in a sound body."

XXI. ETHICS. Will the complete adaptation of perfect external conditions develop the highest moral power? Is that teaching which does not conform to the laws of growth immoral?

PEDAGOGICS.

Professional Training Class.

First Term.

I. Discussion of the Subjects of Study and their relation to each other and to the whole: Geography, geology, mineralogy, physics, chemistry, botany, zoology, anthropology, ethnology and history—unity of studies found in the investigation of laws.

II. Relation of form and number as modes of thinking and means of studying subjects.

III. Relation of oral and written language to the study of subjects. Function of symbols.

IV. Modes of Study or Attention.
   a—Observation. b—Hearing language. c—Reading.

V. Modes of Expression as means of intensifying thought.
   a—Gesture and voice. b—Music. c—Making. d—Modeling. e—Painting. f—Oral language. g—Written language.

   First Hypothesis: Is it possible under adequate teaching and training skill for pupils to acquire all the forms required for thought expression in each and every mode under the immediate impulse of intrinsic thought?

   Second Hypothesis: Is it a necessity under the best teaching and training skill to acquire the technical forms of expression without immediate attention to their highest use, for the purpose of using them afterwards in the expression of thought?

VI. Definitions of Education; teaching, training, principles, methods.

VII. Theory of concentration carefully considered. Economy of human action in the direction of development. Induction and deduction.

VIII. Study of the spontaneous activities of the child. What subjects does every child instinctively study?

IX. Relation of the study of the sciences to geography and history; and to human development.

X. Special Study of the Modes of Attention.
   a—Observation. b—Hearing language. c—Reading. How does a child learn to talk? Elements of speech. Could a child learn to read as he has learned to hear language if the proper conditions were presented?

Second Term.

XI. Special examination of the devices used in teaching reading.
   a—Alphabet. b—Phonic. c—Phonetic. d—Word building. e—Reading-writing method. f—Object method. g—Thought method. h—Laws of the instantaneous synthesis of individual concepts. The devices by which these laws are violated.

XII. Special examination of number and arithmetic teaching.
   a—Method of concentration. b—The five operations. c—Proper function of symbols in teaching arithmetic

XIII. Study of methods of teaching form and geometry.

XIV. SPECIAL STUDY OF THE MODES OF EXPRESSION and their relation to mental development.
 a—Gesture and voice. *b*—Music. *c*—Making. *d*—Modeling. *e*—Painting. *f*—Drawing. *g*—Speech. *h*—Writing. The special function in mental development of each mode of expression.

XV. PEDAGOGICS OF ORAL LANGUAGE.
 a—Speech. *b*—Voice. *c*—Inflection. *d*—Accent. *e*—Emphasis. *f*—Melody and harmony. *g*—Articulation. *h*—Enunciation. *i*—Pronunciation. *j*—Elocution.

XVI. PEDAGOGICS OF WRITTEN LANGUAGE.
 a—Writing. *b*—Spelling. *c*—Punctation. *d*—Capitalization. *e*—Etymology. *f*—Syntax. *g*—Rhetoric.

XVII. EXAMINATION OF PENMANSHIP.
 a—Law of ease. *b*—Accuracy. *c*—Legibility.

THIRD TERM.

XVIII. SPECIAL DISCUSSION of methods of teaching.
 a—Geography. *b*—Science. *c*—History and literature.

XIX. PRINCIPLES AND METHODS OF TEACHING.

XX. SCHOOL MANAGEMENT AND GOVERNMENT.
 a—Motive. *b*—Work. *c*—Courage. *d*—What is order?

XXI. MORAL EDUCATION.
 a—Is all true education moral? *b*—Does all imperfect teaching degrade the pupils taught?

XXII. DISCUSSION OF THE COURSE OF STUDY.

XXIII. HOW TO CRITICISE A SCHOOL.

XXIV. PREPARATION OF LESSONS. Knowledge and skill necessary for a teacher. How to study.

XXV. HOW TO CONFORM TO CIRCUMSTANCES AND STILL MAKE PROGRESS.

HISTORY OF EDUCATION.

Professional Training Class.

EXPLANATIONS.

Taken in its broadest meaning the history of education comprehends the history of the growth, development and evolution of the entire human race. In this sense anthropology, ethnology, philology, the history of architecture and invention, together with history proper, are included in the history of education.

In a more limited and more common definition, the history of education is limited to the evolution of principles and methods of education as originated by men and illustrated and applied in schools.

Under the latter meaning, the history of education begins when purpose and design in developing human beings began; under the former a knowledge of spontaneous human activities with little or no design, and no thoughtful guidance, is related to purpose and design as unconscious is to conscious action. These two meanings have no sharply defined boundaries, one merges into the other as savage and barbarous life evolves into civilization, and as civilization lapses into the methods of barbarism.

This course of study proposes the study of education under both definitions. The study of all history is in reality the history of education.

FIRST TERM.

I. EDUCATION BEFORE THE CHRISTIAN ERA.

    a—Savages. *b*—Barbarians. *c*—Chinese, Confucius. *d*—Egyptians. *e*—Semites. *f*—Aryans. *g*—Ancient Classic Nations, Greece and Rome—Socrates, Plato, Aristotle, Quintillian.

II. THE EARLY CENTURIES after the beginning of the Christian Era.

    a—Previous to the Crusades. *b*—Following the Crusades. *c*—Before the fall of the West Roman Empire. *d*—Up to the time of Charlemagne. *e*—The middle Ages from the time of Charlemagne. *f*—The Mahomedans, the Arabians.

III. THE SCHOLASTIC PERIOD.

    a—Immediately following the Crusades. *b*—Education up to the first quarter of the sixteenth century. *c*—The humanists—Sturm, Ratich, Francke.

SECOND TERM.

IV. THE PHILANTHROPINS.

    a—Comenius. *b*—Basedow. *c*—Rousseau. *d*—Pestalozzi. *e*—Diesterweg. *f*—Fichte.

V. THE REALISTS.

    a—Bacon. *b*—Locke. *c*—Spencer.

VI. FOUNDATION OF A THEORY OF EDUCATION.

    a—Herbart. *b*—The Herbartian Theory. *c*—Ziller, Stoy and Rein. *d*—The Lehr Seminar at Jena.

VII. HISTORY OF THE KINDERGARTEN.

    a—Froebel. *b*—Baroness Von Bulow. *c*—Elizabeth Peabody. *d*—Susan Blow. *e*—Mrs. Quincy A. Shaw.
Development of the Kindergarten in America.

VIII. SECONDARY EDUCATION.

    a—Universities. *b*—Colleges. *c*—Academies. *d*—High Schools.

THIRD TERM.

IX. ORIGIN AND GROWTH OF THE COMMON SCHOOLS OF AMERICA.

    a—Horace Mann. *b*—Henry Barnard. *c*—Thaddeus Stevens. *d*—John D. Philbrick. *e*—Andrew J. Rickoff. *f*—Dr. William T. Harris. *g*—The beginning of the Common School System in different States.

X. ORIGIN AND PROGRESS OF NORMAL SCHOOLS.

    a—James G. Carter. *b*—David P. Page. *c*—Father Pierce. *d*—Tillinghast. *e*—E. A. Sheldon and the Oswego Normal School. *f*—A. G. Boyden and the Bridgewater Normal School. *g*—State Normal Schools. *h*—City Normal Schools—Anna C. Brackett. *i*—Chairs of Pedagogics in colleges and universities.

XI. RECENT EDUCATIONAL MOVEMENTS AND REFORMS.

    a—Art—Walter Smith. *b*—Manual Training—Dr. Otto Saloman, Woodard, Ham, Compton, Runkle. *c*—Teaching of vocal music—Lowell Mason.

XII. HISTORY OF METHODS.

    a—Science. *b*—Geography—Humboldt, Ritter, Guyot, Peschel. *c*—History and Literature. *d*—Modern Languages—Hamilton, Saver, Heuness, Gouin. *e*—Physical Training—Guts Muths, Father Jahn, Ling. *f*—Primary Reading—Ickelsamer, Graser, Jacotot, Bohme, Webb, Pitman, Leigh, Farnham. *g*—Number—Bohme, Warren Colburn, Grube. *h*—Grammar and Language teaching—Ascham, Murray, Green, Stickney.

XIII. PRESENT CONDITION OF EDUCATION.

    a—Germany. *b*—France. *c*—Great Britian. *d*—Italy. *e*—Russia. *f*—Scandinavia. *g*—Belgium. *h*—Denmark. *i*—America.

LANGUAGE.

Practice School.

FIRST GRADE—FIRST TERM.

SPEECH.—Enunciation, pronunciation, slow pronunciation. (Five minute exercises three or four times each day.)
SYNTAX.—Correct continually all mistakes in the use of language.
WRITING.—Write words and sentences used in all lessons upon blackboard; erase and have pupils write from memory. Allow no slow writing. Adapt the words and sentences to be written to the ability of the child.
PENMANSHIP.—Practice ease and rapidity in pen movement. First, practice upon blackboard; second, upon unruled paper; third, upon ruled paper with pencil and pen; fourth, write words and sentences upon paper and upon the blackboard.

FIRST GRADE—SECOND TERM.

SPEECH.—See directions for first term. Make notes of the mistakes in idioms of each pupil. Eradicate these mistakes by training pupils to use correct language. Continue slow pronunciation; relate slow pronunciation to written words. (See course of reading.)
WRITING.—Continue practice upon the blackboard. Write sentences that occur in all lessons upon the blackboard; erase and have pupils write them upon the blackboard. Train pupils to write rapidly and accurately from the first. Begin writing original sentences upon the blackboard. Drills in perfect ease in pencil and pen holding. Write sentences upon paper.

FIRST GRADE—THIRD TERM.

SPEECH.—See directions in previous terms. Continue slow pronunciation. Write list of words in phonic order, and have pupils pronounce them slowly. Give special attention to enunciation, articulation and pronunciation. Correct all mistakes in the use of idioms.
WRITING.—Continue practice upon blackboard and paper. Cultivate the habit of expressing orally and by rapid and easy writing the thoughts evolved in all lessons. Analyze sentences written on the blackboard, by questioning. (See Suggestions and Directions in Teaching Language.)

SECOND GRADE—FIRST TERM.

SPEECH.—Follow carefully all previous directions. Continue slow pronunciation. Write lists of words in phonic order and have pupils pronounce them slowly, with very little aid from the teacher. Cultivate correct and fluent oral expression in all lessons. Practice oral spelling incidentally.
WRITING.—Continue writing upon the blackboard, and upon unruled and ruled paper. If teachers have failed in training pupils to write whole words and sentences with ease, correctness and rapidity, drill pupils in writing single words and letters. Order of small letters: i u w x z v n m t l b h k e o c a d g j y g p f r s.

SECOND GRADE—SECOND TERM.

SPEECH.—Follow every detail already given in the course. Give pupils countless opportunities to observe, examine and investigate in all lessons, and have them express their thoughts orally and by writing. Cultivate sedulously correct language. Continue slow pronunciation, and have pupils write upon the blackboard list of words in phonic order.
WRITING.—Practice upon capitals, if necessary. Order of capitals: A N M H K T F S L P B R G I J O E C D V X Z Q Y U W. The habit of holding crayon, pencil and pen easily is of the first importance. Have pupils write frequently. Have short exercises. Never allow a pupil to write unwatched, until he can be trusted to write correctly. Train pupils to distinguish in writing, between common and proper nouns.

SECOND GRADE—THIRD TERM.

SPEECH.—Make a record of all mistakes committed in pronunciation and syntax by each pupil, and correct them. Use oral spelling to aid the writing. Continue slow pronunciation with lists of words upon blackboard and paper, if necessary.
WRITING.—Write sentences upon the blackboard, used in all lessons; erase, and have pupils write them immediately from memory upon blackboard and paper. Have short exercises, and many of them.

THIRD GRADE—FIRST TERM.

SPEECH.—Begin with pupils just where you find them in skill and ability, without regard to course in grade. Study and apply all previous directions, when necessary. Train pupils to express thought orally, clearly, distinctly and grammatically in all lessons. Use oral spelling in close relation to writing. Write words and sentences upon the blackboard; erase, and have pupils spell them orally. Continue slow pronunciation. Write lists of familiar words that pupils have never seen in print, and have pupils pronounce them.
WRITING.—Continue practice in word and letter writing upon blackboard and paper, if necessary. Have pupils read (silently) short interesting stories, and then write them on paper. Train pupils to distinguish common and proper nouns, also the singular and plural number in spelling.

THIRD GRADE—SECOND TERM.

SPEECH.—Study all directions for previous grades. The teacher should sedulously cultivate quick ear and eye for all mistakes.

WRITING.—Special drill three or four times a day in pen movement, if necessary. Beautiful and rapid penmanship by the teacher will save half the time on the part of the pupils. Have pupils write original sentences, paragraphs and pages. Never trust pupils to write without careful watching. If they do not write accurately. Train pupils in the spelling of the singular and plural number of nouns, and in the writing of the possessive case. Continue analysis of sentences by questioning. Begin the use of the dictionary. Teach diacritical marks.

THIRD GRADE—THIRD TERM.

SPEECH.—Apply carefully, when necessary, the directions already given. Eradicate all mistakes in syntax by constant use of correct language. Use slow pronunciation for the correction of faults in enunciation and pronunciation.

WRITING.—Give dictation lessons to correct bad habits of writing and spelling. Spell words orally, and have pupils write them, if necessary. Continue letter writing, unless pupils can write rapidly and legibly without such exercises. Train pupils to use the dictionary. Write letters with diacritical marks upon the blackboard as a means of learning to use the dictionary.

ETYMOLOGY.—Train pupils to distinguish in reading lessons, nouns (common and proper), the number of nouns, and the possessive case. Write on the blackboard lists of the regular and irregular verbs.

FOURTH GRADE—FIRST TERM.

SPEECH.—Follow strictly all directions given for previous grades, when necessary.

WRITING.—Smooth lines, ease and rapidity are indispensible in writing; make these requirements of the first importance, and then continually and persistently improve in form and legibility. Have many exercises in thought expression by writing. Correct pronunciation by slow pronunciation.

ETYMOLOGY.—Nouns (common and proper), number, personal pronouns. Use the dictionary.

SYNTAX.—Analysis of sentences by questions. Teach pupils to distinguish subjects of sentences, and the agreement of forms of the verb with the nominative case.

FOURTH GRADE—SECOND TERM.

WRITING.—If the work in the previous grades has been effectually done, your pupils can write easily, rapidly and legibly. If the work has not been done, you must begin all over again and strive to correct bad habits. The writing of pupils should be automatic, and at the same time legible. Short and frequent exercises in thought expression. Dictation exercises, if necessary. Train pupils into absolute accuracy.

ETYMOLOGY.—Have pupils recognize at sight, common and proper nouns, the numbers of nouns, personal pronouns, their number and case.

SYNTAX.—Continue analysis by questioning. Have pupils recognize subject and predicate in sentences, and the form/agreement of predicate with subject.

FOURTH GRADE—THIRD TERM.

COMPOSITION.—Compositions should consist of rapid, accurate and legible written expressions of thought evolved in the teaching of all subjects. The penmanship should be easy, rapid, accurate and legible, so that it can be used at all times as a means of developing and intensifying thought. Oral spelling, writing lists of words and dictation, when necessary. Habits of accuracy in spelling, use of capitals and punctuation must be rigidly and persistently cultivated.

ETYMOLOGY.—Nouns (common and proper), number, person, case and gender of nouns and pronouns to be taught as forms of the written expressions of thought.

SYNTAX.—Analysis of sentences by questioning. Subject, predicate and adjective modifiers of subjects.

FIFTH GRADE—FIRST TERM.

COMPOSITION.—Make a marked distinction between pupils who write accurately, and those who must be watched and persistently trained into habits of accuracy. All lessons are to be reproduced, either partially or wholly, by composition.

RULES.—Whenever any rule of orthography, etymology or syntax will assist pupils in the expression of thought, write the rule upon the blackboard and have pupils use it.

ETYMOLOGY.—Teach nouns, person, number, gender, case and adjectives. Teach verbs and adverbs. All teaching of grammar must be in the closest relation to that composition and reading, made necessary by all lessons.

SYNTAX.—Continue analysis. Analysis has for its purpose the closest possible discrimination of thought, expressed by written or printed language.

FIFTH GRADE—SECOND TERM.

COMPOSITION.—Progress in composition is marked by the ease, accuracy, rapidity and legibility, by which a pupil puts his thought upon paper. It is also marked by continually improving legibility, gained only by the ability to make smooth lines rapidly. Expression of thought by writing should be a very important factor in all lessons. Pupils should be ready to write instantly.

RULES.—Whenever a rule of language, orthography, etymology or syntax will aid pupils in the expression of thought, write the rule upon the blackboard, and have pupils learn and use it.

ETYMOLOGY.—Teach verbs, adjectives and adverbs.

SYNTAX.—Analysis of simple sentences. Train pupils to use the dictionary.

FIFTH GRADE—THIRD TERM.

COMPOSITION.—Dictation drills, when necessary; oral spelling to be used as an aid in spelling, proper, or written spelling. For subjects of composition, see "Suggestions and Directions for Teaching Language." The opportunities for teaching composition are countless; the teacher should know how to use them.

SYNTAX.—Analysis; modifying phrases and clauses; conjunctions and prepositions.

RULES.—Have pupils learn and use all the rules immediately necessary for better thought and accurate expression.

SIXTH GRADE—FIRST TERM.

SYNTAX.—Analysis of sentences found in the literature read and studied.

ETYMOLOGY.—Ability to distinguish all the parts of speech in the literature read and studied.

COMPOSITION.—Make writing and speech of equal importance in the evolution of thought. Continue the training into ease, rapidity and legibility of penmanship.

Use every possible means to correct defects in individual pupils. Study carefully, and apply all previous directions in this course, when necessary.

SIXTH GRADE—SECOND TERM.

SYNTAX.—Continue analysis of sentences. All true analysis of sentences is analysis of thought. The thought analyzed should be directly related to the subjects of thought.

COMPOSITION.—The examination of the work done in the study of the subjects should be reviewed by writing. The tests of improvement in composition are enhanced legibility, accuracy, ease and rapidity, and also the amount of writing that can be done in one period.

EXAMINATIONS.—Have frequent written examinations.

ETYMOLOGY.—Relative pronouns.

Highest test of all character is trustworthiness.

SIXTH GRADE—THIRD TERM.

SYNTAX.—Analysis of selected literature. Analyze thought by quickly discerning subjects, predicates and modifiers.

ETYMOLOGY.—Review of parts of speech.

COMPOSITION.—Dictation drills, when necessary. Oral spelling to be used in aid of accuracy in writing.

DERIVATION OF WORDS.—Elementary lessons in the derivation and history of words.

RULE.—Use any rule necessary for the immediate expression of thought.

SEVENTH GRADE—SECOND TERM.

SYNTAX.—Teach the most practical rules of syntax. Continue analysis. Parse sentences in literature, read and studied.

COMPOSITION.—See previous directions.

DERIVATION OF WORDS.—Meaning of prefixes and suffixes. Dictation drills, oral spelling, and drills in spelling lists of words, if necessary.

SEVENTH GRADE—THIRD TERM.

SYNTAX.—Analysis of literature read and studied.

COMPOSITION.—Nearly seven years' drill and practice in writing should give pupils great skill and readiness in composition. The principal work of the teacher now is to remedy defects.

EIGHTH GRADE—FIRST TERM.

GRAMMAR.—A review of all work done in previous grades. Use of "Meiklejohn's English Language." Review of parts of speech and their relations.

DERIVATION OF WORDS.—Guide, "Meiklejohn's English Language."

COMPOSITION.—See all previous instructions in this course. Dictation drills, oral and written spelling, when necessary.

EIGHTH GRADE—SECOND TERM.

GRAMMAR.—Review of analysis. Use of text book.

DERIVATION OF WORDS.—Use of text book.

COMPOSITION.—Continued.

EXAMINATIONS.—Have written examinations frequently. Pupils of this grade should be able to write very rapidly and accurately, and at the same time express profitable thought. All lessons and topics should be reviewed by writing.

EIGHTH GRADE—THIRD TERM.

GRAMMAR.—To be taught in connection with literature. All practical rules of grammar are to be practically acquired.

COMPOSITION.—Rules for composition and the simple rules of rhetoric.

REVIEW.—Review and strengthen the work of the entire course.

READING.

Practice School.

FIRST GRADE—FIRST TERM.

PREPARATION.—Prepare pupils, very carefully, for the first steps of learning to read, by exercises in gymnastics, music, modeling, painting and drawing; also by elementary lessons in science, history and literature (stories).

The power of attention must first be cultivated. Make the transition from hearing language and speaking, to reading and writing, as unconscious as possible. Keep pupils perfectly unconcious of difficulties.

FIRST STEPS.—Write words, and afterwards sentences, upon the blackboard when pupils are intensely interested in the thought expressed by the words and sentences.

WRITING.—Erase the words written upon the blackboard, and have pupils write them upon the blackboard. Encourage the crudest attempts. Have pupils read orally what they write.

PHONICS.—Pronounce slowly, names of objects near at hand and have pupils touch or point to the objects.

FIRST GRADE—SECOND TERM.

PREPARATION.—Make the basis of all reading and writing exercises simple and elementary lessons upon science, history and literature (stories), and training in music, modeling, painting and drawing.

Begin the first steps when the pupil's mind is ready to attend to written words.

SCRIPT READING.—Write words upon the blackboard, erase and have pupils tell what you wrote. Introduce new words under the stimulus of intense interest. Always write sentences when pupils can read them easily.

WRITING.—Make a great difference between pupils who are quick and attentive and those who are slow. Be very careful not to discourage the latter.

PHONICS.—Lead pupils to pronounce simple words slowly.

PRINT —Begin reading print just as soon as the pupils, or group of pupils, read easily from the blackboard, and are capable of taking the important step. Exact indications of readiness to begin print cannot be given, the teacher must decide with each pupil.

SCRIPT.—Continue lessons upon the blackboard. Have lessons in print and writing closely related. Have pupils write upon the blackboard and paper what they read in print. Lead pupils to continually improve their writing in ease, rapidity and legibility Short exercises in easy pencil and pen movements.

ATTENTION.—Cultivate assiduously the three modes of attention: Observation, hearing language and writing. Relate the modes of attention in every lesson and exercise. Have pupils tell what they observe, write what they observe, and read about that which they observe. Have pupils tell what they hear, write what they hear, and read about that which they hear. Have pupils read what they write.

ORAL READING.—When pupils begin to read from print, do not limit their reading to anything, except their actual ability to read. Give pupils plenty of interesting and profitable reading matter.

PHONICS.—Continue slow pronunciation. Have pupils pronounce words slowly. Also relate the slow pronunciation to writing and reading. Write lists of words in phonic order and have the pupils pronounce them slowly.

SECOND GRADE—FIRST TERM.

PREPARATION.—All exercises in reading and writing should spring directly from the thought evolved in all lessons. When a new (to a pupil) oral word is used as a necessity of thought expression, it should be written immediately upon the blackboard.

Three means of intensifying thought in reading:
1. Telling the thought in the pupil's own words.
2. Expressing the thought by writing.
3. Oral reading.

Adapt the means to the ability of the pupil.

CONCENTRATION.—Have all the reading (if possible) concentrated upon the subjects taught.

PHONICS.—Continue slow pronunciation. Write lists of words in phonic order and have pupils pronounce them slowly.

SECOND GRADE—SECOND TERM.

SUGGESTION.—Whenever a pupil can read a selection (silently) and cannot express the thought in the words of the author or is obliged to struggle too much, in attempting to read orally, always lead him to express the thought in his own language. Have pupils write that which they read, using their own language.

DESK AND HOME READING.—Give pupils plenty of interesting reading in school and at home and require them to tell what they read.

PHONICS.—Have pupils write lists of words in phonic order, and then have the pupils pronounce them slowly.

SECOND GRADE—THIRD TERM.

PHONICS.—Correct indistinct enunciation and mistakes in pronunciation by slow pronunciation. Write lists of words in phonics and have pupils pronounce them.

TESTS OF PROGRESS.—Pupils in this term should be able to read with ease good selections in any first reader. Limit their reading matter only to their ability to read (silently).

LITERATURE.—Train pupils to read orally and to recite some fine selections in literature; one selection each month.

THIRD GRADE—FIRST TERM.

PREPARATION.—All the reading matter should grow out of the necessity found in teaching subjects.

PHONICS.—Pupils should be able to pronounce slowly any word pronounced by the teacher and written upon the blackboard.

WRITING.—Have pupils write, in their own language the lessons read.

TALKING.—Have pupils tell what they read in their own language.

ORAL READING.—Have pupils read orally those selections in which they can express the thought by reading orally with ease and good elocution.

THIRD GRADE—SECOND TERM.

CONCENTRATION.—Teach by writing all words evolved in all lessons.

PHONICS.—Test the ability to pronounce readily words that pupils have never before seen in print.

ORAL READING.—Never allow a pupil to read a sentence orally that he has not first read (silently). Demand natural reading. Natural reading springs directly and unconsciously from the instantaneous impulse of thought. Correct all mistakes without impeding the thought action.

TALKING.—Train pupils to read (silently) with rapidity, *i. e.*, to grasp the thought without thinking of the words.

LITERATURE.—Study carefully one fine selection of poetry or prose each month.

THIRD GRADE—THIRD TERM.

TEST OF PROGRESS.—The ability to read orally at sight, good selections from any second reader.

SILENT AND HOME READING.—Furnish pupils with plenty of reading matter, and have them tell you what they read.

Three means of watching mental action in teaching reading:
  Writing, talking and oral reading.
Watch closely your pupils' conscious activities.

FOURTH GRADE—FIRST TERM.

STUDY with great care all the preceding directions in this course. Apply that which is needed by individual pupils, without regard to directions for this grade. Never take any results for granted. The ability and power of the pupil are the only results which should determine the next step with him.

WRITING.—Train pupils to reproduce by writing, the thought acquired in reading.

TALKING.—Have pupils read (silently) as quickly as possible, a story or a description, and then have them tell what they have read.

ORAL READING.—Never allow pupils to try to express a thought by oral reading, until they have the thought to be expressed.

FOURTH GRADE—SECOND TERM.

MOTIVE IN ORAL READING.—Develop the motive in pupils of giving the thought to others, of making those around them understand what they are reading. For this purpose it is a good plan to have all pupils, except the reader, close their books and listen. Call on pupils who have been listening, to tell what they have heard. For the purpose of developing the right motive it is a profitable device to have only one book, and that an interesting story or description.

CONCENTRATION.—So far as possible, have all the reading bear directly upon the subjects taught.

TALKING.—When the reading is too difficult for oral reading, have pupils read (silently), and then tell what they read in their own language.

FOURTH GRADE—THIRD TERM.

TEST OF PROGRESS.—The ability to read orally, at sight, any good selection in a third reader.

LITERATURE.—Give special drills in expression, by teaching one excellent piece of poetry each month. If possible, have the selection related to the subjects taught.

SUBJECTS TAUGHT.—Have reading lessons in geography, science and history. All reading should be the best literature.

FIFTH GRADE.—FIRST TERM.

TEST OF ABILITY TO READ.—Have pupils read (silently) a story or description and then have them write the story 2.—Have pupils read (silently) a story or description and then have them tell what they have read.
RELATION OF READING TO SUBJECTS.—Make your selections for reading from the subjects taught, history, geography, arithmetic and science.
LITERATURE.—Teach one excellent selection of poetry each month.
BACKWARD PUPILS.—Give especial attention to pupils who have hitherto failed to learn to read well. When a pupil stumbles or reads orally without expression, have him drop oral reading for a time; have him read (silently) and then tell what he has read.

FIFTH GRADE.—SECOND TERM.

MODES OF EXPRESSION.—Have continually exercises in writing, speaking and oral reading as means of intensifying the thought, gained by silent reading.
PRONUNCIATION.—Give special lessons in enunciation and pronunciation, when necessary.

FIFTH GRADE.—THIRD TERM.

TEST OF PROGRESS.—(1) Ability to read orally with natural expression any good selection from the fourth reader.
(2) Ability to read (silently) a selection and reproduce the thought by writing.
MOTIVE IN ORAL READING.—Develop strongly in pupils the motive, to make every one within hearing understand the thought expressed.

SIXTH GRADE.—FIRST TERM.

If the teaching of reading has been properly done up to this grade, the reading should be so good, that little or no teaching of reading thereafter, will be necessary. Experience shows, however, that many pupils do not read well after five years' practice. The rule should be, never to continue a bad habit. If a pupil constantly stumbles in oral reading, or reads in a purely mechanical manner, drop all oral reading for a time with him, and train him to read (silently) and tell what he has read either orally or by writing.
STUDY OF TEXT.—The study of text is intensified reading—reading in which the thought becomes clearer and more distinct by closer attention than in ordinary reading. Train pupils to study text, by having them reproduce that which they study, orally and by writing.

SIXTH GRADE.—SECOND TERM.

STUDY.—Use reading as a mode of studying all subjects.
LITERATURE.—Have pupils read and recite one excellent selection in fine literature each month.
CONCENTRATION.—Bring all reading matter to bear upon the enhancement of the subjects taught.
ANALYSIS.—Use grammatical analysis as a means of closely analyzing the thought in reading and studying. Pupils should learn to analyze by closely examining the thought expressed in selections worth studying.

SIXTH GRADE.—THIRD TERM.

STUDY.—The test of reading is the ability to understand the text in all the lessons adapted to the grade.
ELOCUTION.—Drill pupils to read orally, one selection of prose or poetry each month.
TESTS.—Test ability to read by continual exercises in talking, writing and oral reading. The mind will act very quickly in thinking by means of printed language under right training.

SEVENTH GRADE.—FIRST TERM.

ANALYSIS OF THOUGHT.—Use grammatical analysis as a means of close and discriminating thought.
STUDY.—Train pupils to study their lessons, with the closest attention, and then have them tell or write in their own language what they have read or studied.
ELOCUTION.—Select pieces especially adapted to arousing the best emotions in pupils and train them to read (orally) the selections with dramatic expressions.

SEVENTH GRADE.—SECOND TERM.

MOTIVE.—Develop the motive on the part of pupils to make the hearers understand the thought expressed by oral reading.
STUDY.—Continue the close scrutiny of thought by teaching grammatical analysis.
BACKWARD PUPILS.—Do not require oral reading from pupils who have formed habits of stumbling, through fear of pronouncing the words incorrectly. Have such pupils read (silently) and then tell you what they have read. After many exercises in this direction, have them read orally, easy selections.

SEVENTH GRADE—THIRD TERM.

TESTS.—Have pupils study a lesson of several pages for thirty minutes, and then have them tell what they have studied.
ECONOMY OF WORK.—Concentrate all the reading upon the subjects of thought, history, geography, arithmetic and science.
LITERATURE AND LOCATION.—Continue studies of fine literature.
RECITATIONS.—Have pupils learn gems of thought, quotations and beautiful pieces of poetry, and recite them.

EIGHTH GRADE—FIRST TERM.

TESTS.—Test pupils in the quick and clear comprehension of thought by reading and study of text. Test the oral reading by giving pupils selections for silent study, and after sufficient time have them read the selection orally.
ELOCUTION.—All naturalness and power in oral reading, depend upon the unconsciousness on the part of the reader of the words he utters, and his manner and attitude of expression.
STUDY.—Make grammatical analysis a means of comprehending thought. Concentrate all reading upon subjects of study.
TESTS OF POWER IN THINKING BY MEANS OF PRINTED LANGUAGE.—Give short exercises in silent study, and then require pupils to tell or write the thought they have acquired.

EIGHTH GRADE—SECOND TERM.

LITERATURE.—Use excellent literature to cultivate the highest and best emotions. Read that literature which bears directly upon the subjects studied, history, science and geography.
TESTS.—What, and how much, do pupils read without suggestion on the part of the teachers? Is the pupil developing a genuine taste for the best reading? How much original research in books does the pupil make?

EIGHTH GRADE—THIRD TERM.

Eight years of good teaching should give every pupil great power to use printed language as a means of thinking. It should lead to a fine taste in, and great love for good reading and earnest, profitable study. It should give pupils marked power and elegance in oral reading and talking. It should develop great skill in easy, rapid and legible writing. It should have a marked effect upon the character of pupils. It should give them a strong desire to continue study in the high school.

Have these results been accomplished? If not, where are we to lay the blame, how are we to remedy the mistakes?

ELOCUTION AND THE DELSARTE SYSTEM OF EXPRESSION.

Professional Training Class.

FIRST TERM.	SECOND TERM.	THIRD TERM.
Carriage and bearing of the body. Breathing exercises. The Delsarte decomposing exercises. Articulation, enunciation and pronunciation. Analysis of the vowels and consonants: Tables. VOICE: Force, pitch and quality. Reading.	Reading, application of force, pitch and quality. Recomposing exercises.	Reading. Recomposing exercises. Expressive use of the body. Study of the emotions. Pedagogics of elocution.

NUMBER AND ARITHMETIC.

Professional Training Class.

FIRST TERM.

Psychology of number and arithmetic. Relation of number to arithmetic. Relation of number and arithmetic to figures—and to notation and numeration. Number defined. Arithmetic defined. Psychological relation of number to arithmetic. Relation of the mental power of numbering to the knowledge of matter and to energy and its laws, which act through matter.
Relation of number and arithmetic to observation, imagination and processes of reasoning.
Relation of number and arithmetic to properties, qualities and limitations of matter and energy: SIZE, (lines, area, volumes, bulk;) ENERGY, (force, weight, time.)

Ethical relations of number or equivalents of value, (money and substitutes for money).
Relations of number and arithmetic to subjects of thought; geography, science and history.
Relation of number and arithmetic to conceptive modes of expression: music, making, architecture, construction of machinery, utensils, etc.,) modeling, map-making and drawing.
Practical use of number and arithmetic.
Intellectual use of number and arithmetic.
The five operations in number examined and compared: division, partition, subtraction, multiplication and addition.
The factors in each operation defined: What can be done with a number? What can be done with a number of numbers? Operations in numbers and processes with figures thoroughly discriminated.

SECOND TERM.

Derived operations in number.
DIVISION: fractions, decimals, percentage, interest, denominate numbers, ratio and proportion, involution.
PARTITION: fractions, decimals, percentage, interest, denominate numbers, ratio and proportion.
SUBTRACTION: fractions, decimals, percentage, interest, denominate numbers, involution.
MULTIPLICATION: fractions, decimals, percentage, interest, ratio and proportion, evolution.
ADDITION: fractions, decimals, percentage, denominate numbers, processes with figures.
Addition, short and long multiplication, short and long division, subtraction.
Processes with figures in derived operations:—fractions, decimals, percentage, interest, denominate numbers, ratio and proportion, square root, cube root.
Development of automatic remembrance of facts in number and processes with figures.
Investigation of number thinking with subjects of thought, geography, (imagination of dimensions, areas, comparison of heights. Comparison of population, products, etc.)
Science: (weighing, measuring, classifying, force, limitations of time.)
History: (time, dates, epochs, events, etc.)
Use of ordinal numbers, Roman characters.
Investigation of derived operations in number and arithmetic: fractions, decimals, metric system, percentage, interest, denominate numbers, mensuration, ratio and proportion, evolution and involution.

THIRD TERM.

Pedagogics of Number and Arithmetic

FIRST HYPOTHESIS.—Can an adequate knowledge of number and arithmetic be acquired in the study of subjects of thought; science, geography and history together with the exercises necessary for the acquisition of skill in the modes of expression?
SECOND HYPOTHESIS.—Should the facts of number and the processes with figures be acquired by themselves without the closest relation to their practical use, for after use in practical thought; observation, imagination and reasoning?
When should a child begin to learn number?
How should a child begin to learn number?
What general limitations should be made in each grade in the study of number?
Should the five operations be taught together?
Should each operation be taught by itself and not in immediate relation to the other operations?
If so, what should be the order of teaching? Why?
When should figures be taught?
What are the relations of figures to numbers?
What are the psychological processes of adding, subtracting, dividing, multiplying with figures?
What are the differences between the operations of division and partition?
What are the figure differences between the figure processes of division and partition?
How should language be developed by teaching number and arithmetic?
What is the logical arrangement for teaching of the operations—(fractions, decimals, etc.), derived from the five fundamental operations?
Is the usual arrangement of these derived operations pedagogical?
Discussion term by term of the course of study in number and arithmetic for the Practice School.
What should be the limits of automatic remembrance in numerical facts and processes?

THE LANGUAGE OF NUMBER AND ARITHMETIC.

When should definitions and rules be taught?
Can the pupils be taught to make their own definitions and rules?
What is the use of definitions and rules?
Discuss the practical use of each fundamental and derived operation in number and arithmetic.
Discuss the practical use of processes with figures.
Can number and arithmetic be made intensely interesting to children?

ARITHMETIC.

Operations in Numbers.	No.	Subjects.	First Term.	Second Term.	Third Term.
Division.		Lines.	Estimates or distances, inch, foot and yard. Growth of vines and twigs during a season.	Estimates of distances, rod and chain. Heights of children. Angles and slants of the sun's rays.	Estimates of lengths. Growth of trees, plants and vines. Angles.
Partition.					
Subtraction.		Area.	Estimates of areas, square inch, foot and yard.	Work of the earth-worm on a given area.	Area of the school-room, of garden plot for each child, area given to each seed planted.
Multiplication.		Volume.	Estimates of volumes, cubic inch and foot. Estimates of contents of boxes made in sloyd.	Soil thrown up by earth-worms on a given surface. Cubic yard and load of dirt.	Boxes to hold given area of earth-worm work.
Addition.	1 to 10.				
Fractions.		Bulk.	Estimates of contents of vessels, gill, pint and quart.	Estimates of vessels in gallons. Actual measurements by the children.	Solid and liquid measures. Pint, quart, gallon and peck.
Denominate Numbers.		Weight.	Handling and estimating weight of objects in ounces and pounds.	Comparison of different kinds of soil. Comparison of like bulks of different materials.	Weight of children from term to term. When lightest. Why? Average weight of two or more pupils.
Squares.					
Cubes.		Force.	Relation of boiling point to purity of water.	Expansion of metals, liquids and gases.	Capacity of bodies for heat. Radiation of metals.
Processes with Figures.		Time.	Calendar written on the black-board daily. Length of day and night. King Arthur's candles.	Face of clock, ordinal figures, Roman characters. History of clock. Time, how kept in past and present.	Hour-glass, sun-dial, watch, clock. Average length of day and night.
Ordinal Figures		Values.	Postage stamps and coins. History of money. Pine-tree shillings, iron money and bills.	Cost of material used in school by the children, pens, pencils and paper.	Cost of school books, children's clothing.
Notation.					
Numeration.		Single Things	Insect depredations on plants. Kinds and number of insects, and plants examined during the week.	Temperature averages taken from day to day. Number of hot, wet, warm, cold and mixed days in week, month and term.	Kinds and number of metals and stones studied. Averages of meteorological data.

First Grade

ARITHMETIC—Continued.

OPERATIONS IN NUMBER.	No.	SUBJECTS.	FIRST TERM.	SECOND TERM.	THIRD TERM.
Fundamental Operations.	1 to 20	Lines.	Estimates of lengths of objects in the room. Of parts of the body. Of objects in the school yard.	Estimate heights of children. Length of twigs. Growth of vines. Depth of frost.	Compare lengths added to the twigs of different trees. Estimate distances.
Fractions.		Area.	Estimates of leaves of different kinds. Of work done by the earth-worm on given area.	Estimate area of rectangles and irregular forms. Comparison of leaves of different kinds of trees on school yard with foreign trees.	Estimate area in square rods and chains. Measurements by children in the school yard. Triangles and rectangles.
Decimals.		Volume.	Work of earth-worm on given surface. Comparison of fruits and vegetables.	Cubic inch, foot and yard. Estimates of different shaped vessels.	Boxes to hold soil for seeds. Sloyd work. Given volume require boxes to be made.
Denominate Numbers.		Bulk.	Liquid and dry measurements by the children. Pint, quart, and gallon. Different shaped vessels.	Sirup compared with water and vinegar. Estimates of contents of vessels of different shapes. Actual measurements by the children.	Dry and liquid pint and quart. Estimate amount of seeds collected. Verify.
Squares.		Weight.	Of different substances, estimated by eye and hand of same kinds of materials.	Comparison of same bulk of hard and soft coal, lead and iron.	Weight of wood compared with iron, lead and coal.
Cubes.		Force.	Of water and steam. How used.	Of wind, water, air, steam, and how used by man.	Conduction of heat. Capacity of heat. Sources of heat.
PROCESSES WITH FIGURES.		Time.	Daily calendar on blackboard. Lengths and names of each month. Origin of names.	The week, month and year. Ages of children. Average of two or more.	Number of pulse beats in given time. Compare pulse beats of child with dog's for same time.
Notation. Numeration.		Values.	Cost of food and fruit eaten by children. Cost to send letters in past and present.	Cost of different kinds of food. Of different kinds of clothing.	Silver dollar and paper dollar. Old and new coins and postage stamps.
U. S. Money. Ledger Columns.		Single Things.	Fruits collected for study. Kinds and number of seeds collected. Parts of a nut.	Estimate the number of buds on a twig. Number and kinds of seeds collected. Stars in the dipper.	Examine 25 leaves. Number free from insects' depredations. How many ways used? Average number free from depredations.

SECOND GRADE.

ARITHMETIC—Continued.

THIRD GRADE

OPERATIONS IN NUMBER	No.	SUBJECTS	FIRST TERM.	SECOND TERM.	THIRD TERM.
Fundamental Operations.	1 to 30	Lines.	Estimate distances in school yard. Depth of loam in school yard. Depth of loam to clay and sand.*	Length of school ground, width of school ground. Height of school-room, school building.	Estimate rod, chain, mile and fractions of mile. Height of sand dunes at the lake, in desert.
Fractions.		Area.	Wings of birds compared with butterfly. Leaves of trees at home and abroad.	Estimate and measure plots of ground in the child's garden.	Of irregular forms. Estimate amount of vegetation on given area of garden.
Decimals.		Volume.	Given boxes to make in sloyd. Comparison of clay, loam, sand and gravel. Ancient Walls.	Cubic foot, yard and load of soil. Estimate contents of boxes, all sizes and shapes.	Amount of soil thrown up by the earth-worm on a given area.
Metric System.		Bulk.	Water absorbed by loam, sand, clay and gravel, compared.	Estimate contents of bags and sacks in peck, half-bushel and bushel.	Estimate amount raised in garden from different seeds.
Denominate Numbers.		Squares.	Of same bulk of sand, loam, gravel and clay, compared. Estimate, verify.	Estimate of children's weight. Of two or more. Of whole class.	Compare weight of children with first and second term.
Cubes.		Force.	Comparison of heat absorbed by loam, sand, clay and gravel.	Heat radiated from sand, loam, clay and gravel. Elasticity of air and water.	Specific gravity of iron, lead and coal.
PROCESSES WITH FIGURES. Notation.		Time.	Comparative time taken for given amount of water to percolate through loam, sand, clay, gravel and stone.	Ages of children, trees and twigs, plants and animals. Day of the week. Origin of names.	Growth of twigs in given time. Of grass and plants. Compare distance traveled in given time past and present.
Numeration. Multiplication with two Figures.		Values.	Of children's books, toys and school pencils, pens and paper, paints, brushes, paint boxes, etc.	Cost of seeds, compared with value of articles raised from them. Cost of time spent in garden.	Cost of garden. Value of its proceeds. Cost of clothing, summer and winter compared.
U. S. Money. Cash Book.		Single Things.	Kinds of bugs, birds and butterflies found during term. Stories of travel. Labors of Hercules.	Number and kinds of stones gathered for school work.	Kinds and number of trees found on school ground, in the city and country.

* Seldom if ever is there a time when pupils cannot find a sewer, ditch or cellar, where answers to the questions can be given.

ARITHMETIC—Continued.

OPERATIONS IN NUMBER.	No.	SUBJECTS.	FIRST TERM.	SECOND TERM.	THIRD TERM.
Fundamental Operations.	1 to 100.	Lines.	Estimate lengths and distances. Depth of artesian wells. Length of rivers, river basins.	Estimate distances. Comparative heights of trees in hot temperatures, cold climates. Heights of hills and mountains.	Depth of frosts in different soils. Dip and strike of rocks. Rain fall.
Fractions.		Area.	Burrows of earth-worm on given surface.	River basins. Slopes of river basins. Of delta.	Evaporation of different surfaces.
Decimals.		Volume.	Estimate contents of bins, cisterns and boxes. Irrigation.	Rain fall for week and month. Bricks in fence walls.	Of rectangular solids, cellars, post-holes and cisterns.
Interest.		Bulk.	Wheat, corn, oats, rye and rice per acre.	Water in irrigating ditches. Estimate ice. Melt and verify.	Given amount of different liquids compared.
Percentage.		Weight.	Estimates of given bulks. Verify. Of bushels of wheat, oats, potatoes, etc.	Weight of same bulk of air, gas, water, ice and metals.	Specific gravity of wood, iron and lead.
Square Root.		Force.	Of rivers. Long slope and short slope.	Temperature of body. Of schoolroom.	Temperature of child compared with adults.
Cube Root. PROCESSES WITH FIGURES. Long Division.		Time.	Time of sunrise, sunset. Length of day and night.	Between two successive full moons. How measured by the Indians.	Time between two new moons. Voyage of Pilgrims. Date of voyage.
Multiplication with two Figures.		Values.	Different coins, gold and silver. Coins not now in use. Old coins. Their use in history.	Bank bills. History of bank bills. Greenback.	Cost of school books compared with Third Grade. Cost of clothing and toys.
Subtraction. Cash-book. Day-book.		Single Things.	Number and ways water is removed from the land.	Number and kinds of plants killed by the frost. Not killed. Average number.	Number and kinds of birds returning. Number and kinds remaining over winter.

FOR 8TH GRADE.

ARITHMETIC—Continued.

OPERATIONS IN NUMBER.	No.	SUBJECTS.	FIRST TERM.	SECOND TERM.	THIRD TERM.
Fundamental Operations.		Lines.	Comparison of length of rivers, coast lines, and political divisions of North America. Length of parts of the body.	Rain fall of all parts of North America compared with South America. Growth of vines, twigs and trees.	Comparison of length of rivers, coast lines and political divisions of South America. Heights of children. Estimates. Verify.
Fractions.		Area.	Comparison of area of river basins, of North American lakes. Political divisions. Continental drainage. Rectangles and triangles.	Comparison of river basins of South America with each other and with North America.	Comparison of rain fall of North and South America. Average depth of frost in different countries at different seasons, on given areas.
Decimals. Percentage.	1 to 500	Volume.	Contents of silt sent down by great rivers. Rectangular solids and cylinders.	Comparison of lakes, political divisions and rivers of South America. Work of earth-worm on given area. Skyd. Boxes to contain given amounts.	Estimate, verify, amount of air in the room per pupil.
Ratio and Proportion.		Bulk.	Waters of North American continent in rivers, lakes and bay of Niagara river compared with other large rivers.	Waters of lakes and rivers of South America compared with North America.	Contents of mountains, contents of vessels estimated. Vessels of different shapes.
Definitions by Induction. Wood Measure.		Weight.	Estimates of weights of children. Of the same bulk of different material.	Work of the earth-worm during a given time on a given space.	Specific gravity of hard and soft coal, of iron, lead and other materials.
PROCESSES WITH FIGURES.		Force.	Elasticity of air, water and gas.	Expansion of water.	Gunpowder. How used.
Notation. Numeration. Long Division.		Time.	Ages of children. Of men known in history. Explorations of Norsemen. Beginning and ending of the crusades. Columbus, Vasco de Gama.	First use of geographical knowledge of the ancients. Mariner's compass. Explorations of Cortez and the Aztecs.	First use of gunpowder, printing press. Explorations of King Henry of Portugal. Explorations of Pizarro and the Incas, Balboa, DeSoto and Ponce de Leon.
Partition. Subtraction. Interest.		Values.	Bills and receipts. Value of school ground, desks and other furniture.	Written orders, bills, notes. Value of public buildings in the world.	Book-keeping, containing the cost of each child to the school. Public property in city.
Metric System. Profit and Loss. Percentage.		Single Things.	Kinds of birds, bugs, insects and minerals found.	Kinds and number of animals seen. Parts of animals with their uses.	Kinds and number of animals known but not seen. Number of countries in which found.

FIFTH GRADE.

ARITHMETIC Continued.

OPERATIONS IN NUMBER.	No.	SUBJECTS.	FIRST TERM.	SECOND TERM.	THIRD TERM.
Fundamental Operations.	1 to 10,000	Lines.	Comparison of lengths of rivers of Eurasia with each other and with the rivers of North and South America. Foot, rod and meter.	Comparison of coast lines, heights of mountains, angles of sun's rays of Eurasia with those of North and South America.	Comparison of lengths of rivers, river basins and coast lines of Africa and Australia with each other and with those of the American continents.
Fractions.		Area.	Comparison of areas of North America and South America with Eurasia. Areas of river basins in the three continents.	Comparison of areas of political divisions of North and South America with Eurasia. Board Measure Cylinder.	Comparison of areas of the peninsulas of the North and South American continents with Eurasia. Also of Africa and Australia.
Decimals. Definitions. Bills.		Volume.	Sediment carried by rivers each year. Cubic feet of air per pupil in schoolroom.	Stones in wall, bricks in a wall and building. Boxes of same size filled with different kinds of soil.	Silt of great rivers of each continent compared. Amount of sediment in given time. Sloyd. Envelopes for seeds collected.
Wood Measure		Bulk.	Metric system. Actual work by the children in experiments. Boiling of pure and impure water.	Contents of bins, circular and rectangular cisterns. Both systems	Amount of water in given time carried by rivers, studied by the children. Both systems to be used.
PROCESSES WITH FIGURES.		Weight	Comparison of different kinds of stone, as flint, marble, granite and rock	Of a given volume of different kinds of soil. Boxes containing the soil to be made by the pupils.	Weight of children compared with those taken the first term. Causes of difference found
Commission Stocks		Force.	Specific gravity of minerals.	Expansion of air, water and other liquids.	Elasticity of different kinds of substances studied by the children
Compound Interest.		Time	Date of first frost, snow, and depth of snow and frost at different times. Colonial wars. Settlements of thirteen colonies.	Confucius' birth and work. Marco Polo, Cyrus, Puritans, Thanksgiving. The Royal Colony.	Date of Lord Clive, Mogul Empire, Plymouth Company, Roger Williams, Quakers, William the Silent, Hudson, Washington, Calvert, Lord Baltimore.
Bank Discount Book-keeping.		Values	Interest. Cost of buildings, brick, stone and lumber.	Cost of school books and other material compared with fifth grade.	Lists of articles with cost as found in grocer's store, dry goods and fancy goods stores.
Bills.		Single Things.	Contrast eastern and western highlands' animals. Domestic animals known. Wild animals.	Kinds of fruit and vegetables in our garden; in our own country. In other countries.	Kinds of seeds found on the school grounds. Seeds found at home.

SIXTH GRADE

ARITHMETIC—Continued.

SEVENTH GRADE

OPERATIONS IN NUMBER.	No.	SUBJECTS.	FIRST TERM.	SECOND TERM.	THIRD TERM.
Fundamental Operations.		Lines.	Comparison of the rivers of the world. Coast lines of continents. Snow line. Distance to different planets.	Heights of mountains. Depths of lakes and oceans. Storm line. Line of directions of center of gravity.	Width of zones. Angles of sun's rays, etc., at different seasons of the year.
Definitions.		Area.	Comparison of continents of the earth. Of deserts. Deltas and river basins. Trapezoid, circle and pentagon.	Comparison of political divisions and of the zones on the earth. Also of deserts and deltas.	Water area of the continents compared with the land area. The same comparison with the world.
Square and Cube Root.		Volume.	Compare sediment of Mississippi river with Amazon river. Contents of irregular forms.	Comparison of pebbles in different parts of the stream. Of trees in different parts of the country.	Excavating cellars, ditches and canals. Irregular forms.
Business Forms.	1 to 1,000,000.	Bulk.	Contents of Cisterns, bins, vats and barrels. Dry and liquid measures.	Compare bulk of water received by the two oceans from North America.	Compare bulk of water received by the two oceans from South America.
Bills.		Weight.	Comparison of same bulk at base and top of mountains. Ton, fractions of a ton.	Troy and Apothecaries weight compared. Weight of coins, metric system.	Of parts of an apple and other fruits. Per cent. of each part found.
Longitude and Time.		Force.	Boiling of water at different altitudes.	Pressure of air. The lever.	Conduction of heat. Electricity.
PROCESSES WITH FRACTIONS.		Time.	Revolutions of the earth. Day and night. Month. New and full moon. Conduction of heat.	Of great events to the present time. Birth of noted men. Explorations.	Vibration of pendulum. History of pendulum.
Promissory Notes.		Values.	Of land in the country compared with city lots. Taxes of county and city compared.	Of railroads. Stocks. Of street car lines. Cost of travel per mile.	Cost of canals of the world. Railroads of the world.
Partial Payments.		Single Things.	Averages of meteorology record for the week, month and term.	Products per acre of different soils. Meteorology averages.	Meteorology averages for the year. Kinds of minerals collected.
Exchange.					
Taxes.					
Book-keeping.					
Bils.					
Longitude and Time.					

ARITHMETIC—Continued.

Eighth Grade.

OPERATIONS IN NUMBERS.	No.	SUBJECTS.	FIRST TERM.	SECOND TERM.	THIRD TERM.
Fundamental Operations.		Lines.	Length of degrees of different parts of the earth, both latitude and longitude.	Angles of the sun's rays in each zone. Distance to the sun, moon and other planets.	Diameter and circumference of the earth in degrees and miles. Of the sun, moon and other planets.
Fractions.		Area.	Comparison of great rain-fall and little rain-fall. Desert area of the world. All forms.	Areas of forests, of grasses, of perpetual snow, of valleys, of mountains, etc.	Area of the white, black and yellow races compared.
Ratio and Proportion.		Volume.	Deposit of silt of rivers in different countries compared.	Of mountains of coal, iron, gold, silver and copper mines.	Gold, salt and lead mines of the world compared.
Definition.	1 to 10,000,000,000.				
Business Forms.		Bulk.	Contents of rivers, lakes, oceans, canals and gulfs of North America. Amount taken in one day by sun.	Contents of rivers, lakes, seas, and gulfs of South America.	Contents of lakes, rivers, seas, and gulfs of Eurasia and Africa.
PROCESSES WITH FRACTIONS.		Weight.	Parts of fruit. Percentage of each part found. Metric system. Green grass compared with dry grass.	Weight of earth. Amount of gold and silver found in cubic yard.	Weight of articles sold by the hundred and ton. Hay to an acre.
Ratio and Proportion.		Force.	Elasticity of water, steam, air and fire, compared.	Gunpowder, dynamite, how made and used.	Actions of sun's rays on a given area. Per cent. of shrinkage of grass and grain.
Denominate Numbers.		Time.	Time since the Hartford convention. Second war with England. Length of Federal party. Missouri compromise.	Time since Monroe doctrine, Nullification, National bank, Whig party, Mexican war.	Time since annexation of Texas, Free-soil party, Omnibus bill, Kansas-Nebraska bill, Know-nothing party, election of Lincoln.
Mensuration.					
All cases in Percentage.		Values.	Value of school material compared with other grades.	Cost of clothing, food, and other living expenses. In summer compared with winter.	Cost of seed per acre. Receipt from seed per acre.
Involution and Evolution.					
Book-keeping.		Single Things.	Classify articles that have taste. Those that have but little taste.	Number and kinds of soil productions. Those that grow under the soil. In the open air.	Kinds of materials, seeds, fruits and stones collected for the school.
Partnership.					

VOCAL MUSIC—PROFESSIONAL TRAINING CLASS.

Music is the highest poetical expression of thought and feeling, and it is in a high degree valuable in fixing thought gained through channels of observation and reason.

The tranquilizing and harmonizing effect of music is very useful in the school room in the blending of various elements of character.

Cultivation of sense of rhythm, and its effect upon the character in the directions of punctuality and order.

Sense of pitch being cultivated quickens observation in realm of sound, and improves the speaking voice.

Singing in its effects upon the body. Beautifying the voice has a reflex action upon the character. The ideal of a beautiful tone ever-present in the mind tends to conceptions of universal beauty. All art is one.

Theory of music necessary to the reading of all songs in one, two, three and four parts. Major and minor scales, their intervals and relations to each other. The triads of each scale tone, and chords of the seventh and ninth found in the major and minor scales. A study of rhythms.

Exercises for gaining thorough control of the breath in singing.

Work in voice culture, to establish the three registers, and to gain a clear, bright, nominal tone. The study of the ideal tone—the tone capable of expressing the beautiful. Its different colorings for the expression of varying thoughts and emotions.

In the singing of songs, which are to be chosen with regard to musical excellence, as well as to fitness of subject, the articulation of the words of the text, and the proper declamation of the same. Phrasing. Musical style.

The entire course in music has for its purpose the preparation of teachers to teach that subject in the common schools of Cook County.

COURSE OF STUDY IN VOCAL MUSIC—PRACTICE SCHOOL.

First Grade—First Term.

Breathing exercises.
Simple exercises in rhythm.
Major scale considered as a unit.
Sections of major scale ascending and descending from tonic (do) as preparative for singing intervals. Skip of the octave.
Simple exercises for limbering jaw.
Songs with special attention to phrasing, declamation and enunciation of text and style. Also to the production of a clear and beautiful quality of tone.

Second Term.

Breathing exercises, exercises in rhythm.
Intervals of second, third, fourth, fifth, sixth and seventh—found between tonic (do) and other scale tones.
Arpeggios of common chord of the major scale (do, mi, sol, do) in three positions.
Exercises for limbering tongue and jaw as before. Songs.

Third Term.

Absolute pitch names: C, D, E, F, etc.
Sing descending passages of five tones (s, f, m, r, d), beginning on G and ascending to E chromatically with mo, ma, may, me,
lo, la, lay, le,
no, na, nay, ne.

Second Grade—First Term.

Introduction of symbols of pitch and length of tones—staff with clef, and the whole note and rest.
Simple reading exercises in key of C.
Exercise for tone-placing—skips of octave with ah-oh, ah-awo and ah-ah.
Breathing exercises and songs.

Second Term.

Intervals found in major scale reckoned from each scale tone separately.
Arpeggios of each triad found in the major scale (do, mi, sol, do), re, fa, la, re; m, s, t, m; f, l, d, f, etc.
Breathing exercises, songs, etc., as before.

Third Term.

Easy exercises in double and triple time.
Accent, time marks, bar and double bar.
Introduction of half and quarter notes and rests.

Third Grade—First Term.

Ascending octaves and descending scales with vowels ah-oh, ah-awe, and ah-ah, for beautifying and evening the middle register.
Analysis of scale—tone and half-tone. G major scale.
Successions of five chromatic half-tones sung as a melody with words, also with syllables.
Songs and breathing exercises.

Second Term.

Reading exercises in quadruple and sextuple time. Eighth and sixteenth notes and rests. The dot. The tie and the hold.
Same voice exercises as before. Songs and breathing exercises.

Third Term.

Scale of D major.
Easy exercises in organ point.
Chromatic half-tones as before, dividing the scale into three sections and singing each separately as a melody.

Fourth Grade—First Term.

A major.
Chromatic scale, ascending and descending, with arpeggios and descending scales.
Keep high voice clear and free and the medium register unmixed with chest tones.
Songs and breathing exercises.

Second Term.

E major.
Easy canons.
Voice exercises, etc., as before.

Third Term.

B major.
Skips from the tonic to different pitches in chromatic scale.
Easy canons.

Fifth Grade—First Term.

Natural succession of clear and somber vowels—e, a, ä, ah, oo, oh, aw, uh.
Exercises in articulation with all vowels and consonants.
Exercises in F and B♭.
Easy part songs.

Second Term.

Key of B♭.
Part songs, voice exercises, songs as heretofore.

Third Term.

Key of E♭. Dynamic signs. Terms, description of tempo and style of singing.

Sixth Grade—First Term.

Arpeggios of dominant seventh chord (sol, te, re, fa), in different positions.
Arpeggios of dominant ninth chord (sol, te, re, fa, la), in different positions.

Second Term.

Staccato and legato. A♭ major scale.
Various seventh chords.
Part songs.

Third Term.

As before.

Seventh Grade—First Term.

D♭ major scale.
Relative minor scales (harmonic).
Two and three part songs.

Second Term.

Intervals of the minor scale.
Contrast of major and minor scales.
Exercises in articulation. Songs and breathing exercises.

Third Term.

Tone coloring. Songs to bring out various qualities of tone.
Arpeggios of various minor chords.

Eighth Grade—First Term.

Melodic minor scale.
Intervals of the same.

Second Term.

Reading exercises in all keys.
Three and four part songs.

Third Term.

Bass clef. Reading in the same.

GEOGRAPHY—PROFESSIONAL TRAINING CLASS.

FIRST TERM.	SECOND TERM.	THIRD TERM.
Definitions of geography. Psychology of observation, imagination and inference in relation to geography. Pedagogics of teaching primary geography. Study of the river basin. Study of characteristic types of surface forms as results of particular geological processes. Structure of South America and North America. Modeling in sand and chalk modeling of all surface forms. Relation of geography to physics. Training of skill in blackboard drawing and modeling.	Study of continents—Eurasia (Europe and Asia), Africa and Australia. Study of island structure. Comparison of continents in structure and drainage. Relation of geography to history: a Effects of geographical environments upon civilization. b Relation of geographical knowledge to memory. Distribution of heat over the earth's surface. Relation of number, arithmetic and form to the study of geography.	Distribution of air: winds; ocean currents. Distribution of moisture; rainfall. Distribution of soil. Distribution of plant life. Distribution of animal life: races of men. Anthropology and ethnology Political geography. Development of civilization. Studies of the geography of China, India, Syria Egypt, Greece, Italy, Spain, Scandinavia and Great Britain in relation to history.

GEOGRAPHY - Practice School.

Grade	MINERALOGY.	GEOLOGY.	STRUCTURE.	METEOROLOGY.	MATHEMATICAL	VEGETATION.	ANIMALS.	POLITICAL.
FIRST GRADE	Pebbles. Sand.	Effect of rain in school grounds. Sedimentation. Wearing of pebbles.	School ground. Mold places described in literature and history.	Wind, clouds, dew, frost. Change of seasons. Effect on plants and animals. Evaporation. Temperature.	Sunset, sunrise. Moon's phases. Directions.	Distrib'n of seeds in this locality. Local vegetation. Effect of heat and cold on vegetation. Mosses, lichens. Growing plants.	Change of animal covering on account of temperature. Migration of birds.	Location of places described in stories.
SECOND GRADE	Rocks and pebbles of different hardness.	Sedimentation Result of freezing and thawing. Effect of water on school grounds.	School grounds and environment. Places visited. Places designated in stories.	Dew, frost, snow, clouds, wind, temperature. Change of seasons. Effect on plants and animals.	Sunrise, sunset. Moon's phases. Horizon.	Distrib'n of seeds in this vicinity. Growing plants. Effect of heat and cold on plants. Fruits, temperate and tropic.	Animals in this locality. Change of covering. Migration of birds.	Location of places in neighborhood; in stories.
THIRD GRADE	River pebbles. Glacial pebbles. Lake pebbles. Loam, gravel. Sandstone. Limestone. Quartz. Sand.	Record changes of surface of soil by wind, frost, water, heat.	Mold and draw school ground and environm't. Islands, capes, promontories, peninsula, gulf, hills, valleys, plains, lowlands, plateau, volcano, beach.	Evaporation, condensation. Direction of prevailing wind. Effect of heat, cold, air, water, soil on plant life. Relation of light, heat, rain, to surface structure.	Place and time of rising and setting sun. Observe rotation of dipper. Moon's phases. Tell time by shadow.	Influence of roots on soil. Decay of vegetation: peat. Difference in growth on north and south side of trees. Fruits, grains.	Animals in this locality. Influence of earthworm, crayfish, ant on soil.	Location of places in history and literature.
FOURTH GRADE	Loam. Sand. Gravel. Sandstone. Limestone. Quartz. Granite.	Changes of lake shore—wearing, building. Delta-flood-plain. Valley. Sand-dunes. Falls. Estuaries.	River basin. All forms of land within river basin; river; lakes.	Effect of heat, cold, air, water, soil, plant life on each other. Relation of clouds, vapor, light, heat to rain. Relation of animals to plants. Action of tillage on soil. Relation of wind to temperature. Process of vegetable decay in wet and dry soil. Drainage. Rivers. Brooks. Springs. Wells. Glaciers.	Places of rising and setting sun. Moon's phases. Variation of noon shadow.	Effect of elevation on plant life. Distrib'n of plants in locality. Fruit. Grain. Trees	Animal preparation of change of seasons. Influence of animals on soil. Relation of animals to plants.	Holland, England, Massachusetts in connection with history.

GEOGRAPHY Continued.

Term.		MINERALOGY.	GEOLOGY.	STRUCTURE.	METEOROLOGY.	MATHEMATICAL.	VEGETATION.	ANIMALS.	POLITICAL.
Fifth Grade.	1	Physical properties of soil. Soils of North America.	Construction of vicinity. Formation of North America.	North America, river basins. With history—Italy, Spain, Portugal, Norway.	Changes of climate in this locality. Prevailing winds. Climate of North America.	Equinox. Degrees of sunrise and set north or south of east and west. Change of noon shadow.	Distribu'n of vegetation of North America.	Animals of North America. Migrat'n of birds. Hibernat'n of animals in vicinity.	General divisions of North America. History — Italy, Spain, Portugal, Norway.
	2	Soils of North America.	Formation of North America.	North America. With history—Peru, Mexico, Florida.	Climate of North America. Drainage.	Comparative decrease and increase of length of noon shadow. Winter solstice.	Hibernation of plants. Plants of North America.	Animals of North America. Effect of cold on animals	History — Peru, Mexico, Florida
	3	Soils of South America.	Formation of South America.	South America, river basins. History England, France.	Winds, temperature, rainfall of South America. Drainage of South America.	Measurem't rays of sun. Length of day. Vernal equinox	Awakening of plant life. Vegetation of South America.	Animals of South America. Return of animals to vicinity.	Divisions of South America. History England, France, Canada.
Sixth Grade.	1	Review formation of North America and South America. History of change of river beds of North America and South America.	Comparative structure of North America and South America. History — England, Virginia.	Climate of vicinity. Barometrical influence on climate. Signal service maps. Climate of North America and South America.	Degrees of sunrise and set north and south of east and west. Measurement of slant of sun's noon rays.	Distrib'n of plant life of vicinity of North America and South America.	Animals of North America and South America.	Divisions of North America, South America. History England, Virginia.
	2	Formation of Eurasia.	Eurasia. History — New York, Carolinas, Georgia, Sweden, China, India.	Winds and rainfall of Eurasia.	Comparative decrease and increase of noon shadow.	General distribution of plant life of Eurasia.	Distribut'n of animals of Eurasia.	Divisions of Eurasia. History — New York, Pennsylvania, Georgia, Sweden, China, India.
	3	Construction of Africa, Australia. Glacial deposits of vicinity.	Africa, Australia. History Persia.	Australia, Africa, Asia. History. Persia.	Climate of Africa and Australia.	Angle of sun's rays compared with length of day.	General distribution of plant life of Africa and Australia.	Animals of Africa and Australia.	Divisions of Australia. History—Persia.

GEOGRAPHY—Continued.

Grade	Term	Mineralogy.	Geology.	Structure.	Meteorology.	Mathematical.	Vegetable.	Animals.	Political.
SEVENTH GRADE	1	Physical properties of animals.	Format'n of continents. Distribution of soils.	Comparison of continents of globe.	Changes of climate in vicinity. Causes of change. Winds and rainfall of earth.	Measure, compare slant rays of sun. Signal service maps.	Vegetat'n of continents.	Animals of continents.	Divisions of all the continents.
SEVENTH GRADE	2	Physical properties of minerals.	Comparative formation of river basins of globe.	Comparisons of river basins of globe.	Winds, rainfall of globe.	Rotation and revolution of earth.	Vegetat'n of continents.	Distribu'n of animals of continents.	Compare divisions of continents. History — Egypt, Chaldea, Phœnicia, Palestine.
SEVENTH GRADE	3	Mechanical constituents of minerals.	History of formation of limestone, sandstone, argillaceous rocks.		Winds, rainfall of globe.	Rotation and revolution of earth.			History — States annexed to Union from Washington's to Lincoln's administration.
EIGHTH GRADE	1	Physical properties of minerals.		Review — structure of world. History — West'n and Southern States.	Review — winds of globe.				Distribut'n of political divisions of world.
EIGHTH GRADE	2	Physical properties of minerals.				Review—Rotation and revolution of earth.	Distribution of vegetation of globe.	Distribu'n of animals of world.	Western and Southern States with Civil War.
EIGHTH GRADE	3	Mechanical constituents of minerals.							Distribu'n of governments of the world.

COURSE IN SCIENCE.

The course of study in elementary science, herewith presented, is founded upon the theory that, from the beginning, through a development along unbroken lines of all his thoughts about nature, the child's horizon should be constantly and symmetrically enlarged; that actual advance is marked only by increasing acuteness in observation, greater exactness in conclusion and more refinement in expression. In early years the child catches but glimpses, real glimpses however, of the great problems presented by nature to the human mind, and they arouse curiosity and arrest attention. To deepen this curiosity into thoughtful interest, to have a care that the child's mind be provided with the good grain of great thoughts rather than the light chaff of little words, is the function of the teacher and the school. Small thought in great type is not the proper nourishment for childhood. In selecting topics, therefore, for this course of study, there has been no hesitation in choosing those which under some other theory of education might seem to be too difficult for elementary work. It must be the constant aim of the teacher to build upon the individual experience of each child, and it is not practicable to show within a useful approximation the work done by each grade. The judgment of the teacher must decide this in each case. Elementary science work properly done will do much to overthrow the chain-gang system of class-work routine and the evils of arbitrary gradation. When the teacher begins to deal with the individual pupil, the school is at once resolved into as many grades as there are pupils, and promotion takes place every day.

Experience would seem to indicate that the economical way to do elementary science work is to provide one room, at least, in each building, with properly constructed tables and other articles of a special equipment. This is far cheaper and in most respects more satisfactory than it would be to equip each room, cumbered as it is with desks and books. The conclusion is also justified that the work must be *quantitative*, as far as possible, from the beginning; that is, the pupil must determine, not approximately, but exactly, the limits of the observation upon which his conclusions are based. It is of the utmost importance, therefore, that the pupils be provided with all practicable means for measuring lengths, areas, volumes, bulk and for weighing small quantities. This makes elementary number work absolutely necessary.

It is the aim of the work done in the primary and grammar grades of this school to have the pupils make an intelligent study of the phenomena of nature, and to render these phenomena intelligible through a carefully selected list of experiments performed in the laboratories. Above the second grade, the work is so planned as to give during each week two regular observation or laboratory lessons, one written lesson, one lesson in drawing, painting, modeling, or making, one in science reading, one lesson by a practice teacher from the Professional Training Class, and one study hour. In the first and second grades, the lessons are shorter and more frequent. With the Professional Training Class, an effort is made to show the relation of the development of the child's mind to its physical environment, and to give some insight as to how the rich materials gathered from the realm of nature may be best utilized as subjects of study.

WILBUR S. JACKMAN.

PROFESSIONAL TRAINING CLASS—PSYCHOLOGY OF SCIENCE WORK.

SENSE–PERCEPTION.	COMPARISON.	GENERALIZATION.
I. CONDITIONS.	I. BASIS.	I. SYNTHESIS.
1. *Objective:* Outside the organism.	1. Objective.	1. Proper selection of data.
(a) Space.	(a) Likeness.	2. Logical arrangement of data.
(b) Time.	(b) Unlikeness.	3. Determination of the organic inter-relations of data.
(c) Force.	2. *Subjective.*	
2. *Subjective:* Within the organism.	(a) The judgment.	II. RELATION TO MENTAL GROWTH.
(a) Sense of touch.	II. RELATION TO MENTAL GROWTH.	1. *Knowledge Value:* Organization into classes according to laws.
(b) Muscular sense.	1. *Knowledge Value:* Formation of concepts.	2. *Disciplinary Value:* Cultivation of the reason.
(c) Sense of taste.	2. *Disciplinary Value:* Cultivation of the judgment.	
(d) Sense of sight.		III. TESTS OF THE CONCLUSION.
(e) Sense of hearing.	III. VALUE OF CONCEPTS DETERMINED.	1. The scope of investigation.
(f) Sense of smell.	1. By correctness of data collected.	2. The number of particulars included.
	2. By the degree of exactness in measurements.	
II. RELATION TO MENTAL GROWTH.	3. By clearness of judgment.	IV. CHECKS.
1. *Knowledge Value:* Collection of data.	(a) Dependent upon heredity.	1. *Analysis:* Testing the general law by special cases.
2. *Disciplinary Value:* Cultivation of the senses.	(b) Dependent upon experience.	2. Trained reasoning power.
	IV. CHECKS.	
III. VALUE OF THE DATA DETERMINED.	1. Repetition by the individual.	
1. By the alertness of the senses—physiological conditions.	2. Average of results obtained by different individuals.	
2. By quality of external forces—physical conditions.		
IV. CHECKS.		
1. Joint action of senses—one confirming another.		
2. Joint action of individuals.		

PROFESSIONAL TRAINING CLASS PEDAGOGICS OF SCIENCE WORK.

SENSE PERCEPTION.	COMPARISON.	GENERALIZATION.

I. MATERIALS.
1. *Of Space.*
  (a) Zoölogy—Animal forms.
  (b) Botany—Plant forms.
  (c) Physics—Forms of solids and liquids.
  (d) Chemistry—Forms of crystals.
  (e) Astronomy—Forms of planets.
  (f) Meteorology—Forms of crystals.
  (g) Geography—Forms of surfaces and areas.
  (h) Geology—Forms of rocks, rock-structure, fossils.
  (i) Mineralogy—Forms of minerals, crystals.
2. *Of Time.*
  (a) Zoölogy—Habits—migration, hibernation, etc.
  (b) Botany—Phases of plant-life.
  (c) Physics } Time limitations of
  (d) Chemistry } natural phenomena.
  (e) Meteorology }
  (f) Astronomy—Units—hour, day, week, etc.
  (g) Geography—Surface changes.
  (h) Geology—Earth history.
  (i) Mineralogy—Rock history.
3. *Of Force.*
  A. Physical.
    (a) Zoölogy—Animal movements.
    (b) Botany—Plant movements.
    (c) Physics—Physical changes.
    (d) Meteorology—Elemental forces.
    (e) Astronomy—Movements and places of planets.
    (f) Geography—Surface action.
    (g) Geology—Earth formation.
    (h) Mineralogy—Crystals.
  B. Chemical.
    (a) Nutrition, excretion, etc.
    (b) Plant physiology
    (c) Chemistry—Chemical affinity.
    (d) Rock dissolving.
    (e) Rock formation.
    (f) Mineral formation.
 	
II. TESTS FOR THE TEACHER'S GUIDANCE.
  1. Method—By the recitation.
  2. Modes—The various modes of expression.
    (a) *Space.*—{ Direct: making, drawing, modeling.
             Indirect: drawing, painting, language.
    (b) *Time.*—Indirect: language, drawing.
    (c) *Force.*—Indirect: language, drawing.
	I. QUANTITATIVE. (Spatial.)
	  A. Modes.
	    1. By Wholes—{ Addition.
	                   Multiplication.
	                   Subtraction.
	                   Division.
	    2. By Partition. (Fractions.)
	    3. By Ratio.
	    4. By Percentage.
	  B. Applications.
	    1. To Quantities in Space.
	      (a) Geometry.
	      (b) Arithmetic.
	    2. To Quantities in Time.
	      (a) Arithmetic.
	    3. To Quantities of Force.
	      (a) Arithmetic.
	
	II. QUALITATIVE. (Non-Spatial.)
	  1. Applications.
	    (a) To colors.
	    (b) To qualities of surface.
	    (c) To savors.
	    (d) To odors.
	    (e) To sounds.
	
	III. TESTS FOR THE TEACHER'S GUIDANCE.
	  1. Method—By the recitation.
	  2. Modes—The various modes of expression.
	    (a) *Space.* (Form and outline.)
	      Direct: making, modeling, drawing.
	      Indirect: painting, writing, oral language.
	    (b) *Time.*—Writing, oral language.
	    (c) *Force.*
	      Direct: making, modeling, drawing, painting.
	      Indirect: writing, oral language.
		I. INDUCTION.
		  1. Inference.
		  2. Judgment.
		  3. Hypothesis.
		  4. Classification.
		  5. Definitions.
		  6. Law.
		
		II. TEST FOR THE TEACHER'S GUIDANCE.
		  1. Deduction.
		    (a) Statement of the hypothesis.
		    (b) Testing the hypothesis by particular cases.

SCIENCE WORK FOR ALL GRADES.

	SEPTEMBER.	OCTOBER.	NOVEMBER.	DECEMBER.	JANUARY.
ZOÖLOGY.	Problems in connection with study of protective coloration of insects and other animals. Insects: Transformations, habits, relation to structure. Earthworms: Habits. Tadpoles: Transformations. Migration. Painting, Drawing, Writing.	Study of Tissues: Determination of ash and organic matter in bone, muscle, etc. Migration. Preparation of ants' nests for winter observation. Painting, Writing, Drawing.	Study of animal coverings. The human skin; functions and structure; comparisons with other animals. Hibernation. Animal warmth.	Animal movements. The bony skeleton. Study of the ratios of the different bones in length to each other. Ratios of human bones to those of other animals by length. Habits of animals still abroad. Drawing, Modeling, Writing.	Study of Foods: (a) Of human beings. (b) Of animals that remain here over winter. Cooking. Hunger. Appetite. Outdoor studies of animals that are to be seen. Writing.
BOTANY.	Fruits: Determination of solid, fluid, mineral and organic constituents; problems in determination of prevailing color and form; problems bearing on relation to animal life. Modeling, Painting, Drawing, Writing.	Fruits—continued: Problems on (a) Plant growths. (b) Distribution of seeds. (c) Insect depredations on different plants. Vegetables raised in school garden. Hardening of wood. Fall of leaves. Modeling, Painting, Drawing, Writing.	Preparation of plants for winter: (a) Leaves. (b) Buds. Effects of frosts. Annuals. Biennials. Perennials. Drawing, Painting.	Effects of freezing on plants. New wood compared with old. Drawing, Writing.	Winter condition of plants: (a) Buds. (b) Twigs. (c) Seeds. Drawing, Writing.
PHYSICS.	Light: Study of spectrum in connection with colors of fruits and animals. Magnetic needle in study of direction. Making, Painting, Drawing, Writing. Problems in plotting and map-making.	Evaporat'n: Problems showing relation to extent of surface and other conditions. The Boiling Point: Problems showing relation of boiling point to purity of water, kind of fluid, etc. Condensation: Applications to natural phenomena. Drawing, Writing.	Heat: Problems relating to expansion of iron, brass and copper. Temperature. Temperature sense. Problems relating to expansion of liquids. Temperature of maximum density of liquids. Expansion of air. Drawing, Writing, Making.	Problems relating to the lever. Application to animal movements. Equilibrium of bodies. Heat: Problems in Conduction. Liquefaction. Convection. Problems in the Capacity of bodies for heat. Sources of heat. Drawing, Writing, Making Apparatus.	Air: Elasticity, pressure. Barometer. Problems on the pendulum. Drawing, Writing, Making Apparatus.
CHEMISTRY.	Fermentation of fruit juices. Tests for carbon dioxide. Yeast action, decay. Writing.	Solution: Problems relating to effect on temperature. Solvents: Saturated solutions. Crystallization: Water of crystallization. Modeling, Writing.	Physical, compared with Chemical change. Problems relating to formation of mixtures and chemical combinations. Tests with lime water and flame for CO_2. Writing.	Preparation of oxygen: Compared with air and CO_2. Experiments showing its properties.	Preparation of hydrogen: Experiments showing its properties. Compared with air, oxygen and CO_2.

75

SCIENCE WORK FOR ALL GRADES—Continued.

	SEPTEMBER.	OCTOBER.	NOVEMBER.	DECEMBER.	JANUARY.
METEOROLOGY.	Daily Record of Meteorological Conditions: Dew, Frost, Direction of Wind, Clouds, Fogs, Rainfall, Snow, Temperature, Air Pressure. Weekly and monthly summaries. Problems derived from data furnished by summaries.	Meteorological Record (see September). Weather Bureau maps. Problems derived from monthly summaries and from comparisons with September. Writing.	Meteorological Record (see September). Weather Bureau maps. Use of Meteorological charts in "Nature Study." Problems as in October.	Meteorological Record (see September). Weather Bureau maps. Problems: See previous months.	Meteorological Record (see September). Weather Bureau maps. Problems: See previous months.
ASTRONOMY.	Daily Record of time of sunrise, sunset, moon's phases, moonrises, moonsets, morning and evening stars, variation in slant of sun's rays, variation in length of day and night. Horizon, equinox. Problems derived from summaries relating to length of day, slant of rays, etc.	Daily Record (see Sept.). Variation of slant of sun's rays; use of shadow-stick. Variation in day's length. Preparation of charts used in "Nature Study." Problems derived from data gathered by observation.	Daily Record (see Sept.). Slant of sun's rays. Day's length. Moon's phases. Comparisons with previous months. Conspicuous constellations.	Daily Record (see Sept.). Topics given in previous month continued. Winter solstice. Comparisons with previous months. Problems derived from summaries and comparisons. Conspicuous constellations.	Daily Record (see Sept.). Work of previous month continued. Movements of planets. Problems as in previous months.
GEOGRAPHY.	Direction. Cardinal points. Horizon, latitude, longitude. Position of North America on the globe.	Drainage of North America. Map modeling and drawing. Field work.	Climate of North America. Isotherms studied. Drainage of South America.	Soils and productions of North America. Climate of South America.	Productions of South America. Modeling, Drawing.
GEOLOGY.	Geological history of surrounding country. Data gathered in field work. Sand modelling. Drawing, Writing.	Erosion and sedimentation. Forms of streams; their channels. Sorting power of water. Rapids, waterfalls. Problems showing the am't of silt in water.	Study of pebbles that have been collected by pupils. History of a pebble as shown by its form and material.	Effects of freezing on soil and rock. Weathering noted on walls and buildings. Problems showing the am't of water absorbed by different kinds of rocks.	Study of conditions which determine the depth to which soil freezes. Study of fossil plant. Conditions of fossilization. Changes in environment involved.
MINERALOGY.*	Physical properties of minerals collected by pupils. Hardness, lustre, color, streak, diaphaneity, form, tenacity.	Study of sand: Formation and deposition. Sand found in soil. Origin of sand.	Mineral fuel. Properties of different varieties of coal. Specific gravity of different varieties.	Determination of specific gravity of minerals. Study of iron ores.	Acid tests applied to minerals. Carbonates. Silicates.

* NOTE.— Records are kept in a specially prepared Record Book.

SCIENCE WORK FOR ALL GRADES—Continued.

	FEBRUARY.	MARCH.	APRIL.	MAY.	JUNE.
ZOOLOGY.	Prehension of food: (a) In man. (b) In other animals. Mastication. Digestion. Outdoor studies. Drawing, Writing.	The circulation of the blood. Nature of the blood; functions. Studies of first signs of spring: (a) Migration of birds. (b) Opening of cocoons in school room since autumn. (c) Preparat'n of Natural History calendar. Writing.	Respiration; function. Structure of lungs and gills. Earthworms. Problems on amount of soil moved. Flight of birds. Collection of insects. Habits of early insects. Pond-life: Frogs, tadpoles. Drawing, Painting, Writing.	The Senses: Care of the eyes and other organs of sense. Birds' nests and eggs. Study of a hen's egg. The crawfish. Painting, Drawing.	Birds: Food, care of their young. Study of feathers and plumage. Insects: Ants, bees, wasps. Reptiles: Snakes, turtles. Review of year. Painting, Drawing, Writing.
BOTANY.	Winter condition of plants: (a) Buds. (b) Twigs. (c) Seeds. (d) Evergreens. Drawing, Writing.	A tree selected by each pupil for special study. Forms of trees. Study of wood and bark. Drawing, Painting, Writing.	Problems showing amount of water absorbed by germinating seeds. Preparat'n of school garden. Study of a seed; compared with a bud. Buds classified. The plant axis: (a) Stems. (b) Roots. Monocotyledons. Dicotyledons. Drawing, Painting, Modeling, Writing.	Study of flowers; function, structure, habitat. Unfolding of buds. Problems showing relation of the number of active to dormant buds. Vernation. Mosses. Painting, Drawing, Writing.	Plant physiology. Problems relating to functions of leaves, stems and roots. Functions of leaves: Structure, arrangement. Exogens. Endogens. Grasses. Grains. Review of year. Drawing, Painting, Writing.
PHYSICS.	Air: The different forms of pumps. The siphon; problems. Capillarity; problems. Buoyancy of liquids; problems. Pressure of liquids. Drawing, Writing, Making Apparatus.	Light: Study of a beam. Seeing: Problems in reflection of light. Images by reflection. Shadows. Drawing, Writing, Making Apparatus.	Light: Problems in refraction. Images by refraction. The prism. Problems in the study of lenses. Drawing, Writing.	Sound; vibration. The Æolian harp. Problems relating to pitch. Communication of sound. Echoes. Music. Drawing, Writing, Making Apparatus.	Magnetism. Frictional electricity. Voltaic electricity. Batteries. Currents. Galvanometer. Review of year. Drawing, Writing, Making Apparatus.
CHEMISTRY.	Study of carbon as obtained from wood, coal, sugar, other forms of carbon. Sources of CO2 considered.	Preparation of nitrogen. Experiments showing its properties. Compared with air, oxygen, hydrogen and CO2.	Water: Mechanical impurities. Hard water. Soft water. Test for salt. Distilled water.	Study of flames: (a) Candle. (b) Alcohol lamp. (c) Bunsen burner.	Chlorine: Preparation, properties, uses. Review of year.

SCIENCE WORK FOR ALL GRADES Continued.

	FEBRUARY.	MARCH.	APRIL.	MAY.	JUNE.
METEOROLOGY.	Meteorological Record (see September). Weather Bureau maps. Problems: See previous months.	Meteorological Record (see September). Weather Bureau maps. Problems: See previous months.	Meteorological Record (see September). Weather Bureau maps. Problems: See previous months.	Meteorological Record (see September). Weather Bureau maps. Problems: See previous months.	Meteorological Record (see September). Weather Bureau maps. Problems: See previous months. Thunder storms. Lightning. Review of the year.
ASTRONOMY.	Daily Record (see Sept.). Topics of previous months continued. Problems as in previous months.	Daily Record (see Sept.). Topics of previous months continued. Vernal equinox. Problems as in previous months.	Daily Record (see Sept.). Topics of previous months continued. Influences of the month upon plant and animal life. Problems as in previous months.	Daily Record (see Sept.). Topics of previous months continued. Movements of planets. Problems as in previous months. Influences of astronomical conditions on life.	Daily Record (see Sept.). Topics of previous months continued. Comparisons with March, December and September. Summer solstice. Problems as in previous months. Review.
GEOGRAPHY.	Relief and drainage of Eurasia. Modeling, drawing.	Climatic influences found in Eurasia.	Productions of Eurasia.	Relief, drainage, climate and productions of Africa and Australasia.	Study of the great wind and ocean currents of the world.
GEOLOGY.	Study of effects of freezing upon soil and rock. Study of a fossil animal. Conditions of fossilization compared with those necessary for fossilization of a plant.	Study of organic forces as geologic agencies. Study of corals.	Study of organic forces as geologic agencies. Field work in the study of swamps.	Study of vicinity by means of field lessons. Rock formation: Stratification, dip, strike.	Study of springs and wells. Location and causes. Field work.
MINERALOGY.	Effects of calcination upon different minerals: Limestone, lime. Gypsum, plaster-paris. Brick-making.	External forms of minerals; tissues, botryoidal form, concretions, stratified, tufaceous, stalactite, stalagmite, crystalline, compact, foliated, fibrous.	Flame tests applied to minerals. Fusibility. Decrepitation. Sodium flame. Sublimation. Tests with litmus paper.	Study of soil as affecting plant life. Mechanical constituents: (a) Coarse gravel. (b) Fine gravel. (c) Coarse sand. (d) Fine sand. (e) Clay, loam. Problems to determine the relative amounts of each in a given sample.	Study of soils as affecting plant life. Physical properties: (a) Absorption and retention of heat and moisture. (b) Evaporation of water from soils. (c) Conduction of heat. Problems on data gathered, making definite comparisons of different samples.

77

HISTORY AND LITERATURE—PROFESSIONAL TRAINING CLASS.

BASIS: The continuity of civilization; opinions, habits and institutions a growth; our age the result of the forces of the past; history a study of causes and results. Periods:—

1. PREHISTORIC.	2. DESPOTISM.	3. GREEK.	4. ROMAN.	5. MODERN.
Ages of savagery and barbarism. Format'n of tribes. Birth and growth of myth.	Oriental idea in government. Early society and religion.	Idea in governm't. Local self-government developed. No centralization. Relation to the Orient.	Idea, "Incorporation without Representation." Relation to Greece and the Orient.	Or Teutonic idea. "Incorpora'n with Representation." Democratic. Relation to all the past.

Cultivation of—

1. OBSERVATION.	2. IMAGINATION.	3. JUDGMENT.	4. MORAL NATURE.
Actual contact with material.	Realizati'n of the past where observation cannot be used.	Discrimination in regard to evidence.	Force of example. Feeling of responsibility developed. Emotions aroused. Tastes directed.

Adaptation of subjects to successive stages of growth. Method—

I. INVESTIGATION.

1. Material:
   a Sources — Geography, monuments, relics, art, records, literature.
   b Authorities.
2. Independent study.
3. Conclusions usually presented in writing.

II. VERIFICATION.

1. Comparison with work of other students in recitation.
2. Discussion.
3. Criticism.
4. Suggestive questioning by the teacher.
5. Presentation of new material by the teacher.
6. Lectures.
7. Enlarged research.

FIRST TERM.

1. Primitive man.
2. Homer's Iliad and Odyssey.
3. Modern authorities on the myth-making age.
4. Oriental nations, or nesting-places of history, as Egypt and Assyria.
5. Beginn'gs of American history; comparisons.
6. Modern poems showing the influence of the myth.

SECOND TERM.

1. Oriental nations, or nesting-places of history, as China, India.
2. Grecian history.
3. Reading of at least one of the dramas of Æschylus and one of Sophocles or Euripides.
4. Roman history.
5. The Age of Virgil.
6. American history, continued.

THIRD TERM.

1. Mediæval history.
2. Dante's Divine Comedy or other studies in the same period.
3. Modern history, including American.
4. Shelley's Prometheus, or other studies in the same period.
5. Studies in the literature of our own age.

HISTORY AND LITERATURE—PRACTICE SCHOOL.

	FIRST TERM.	SECOND TERM.	THIRD TERM.
FIRST GRADE.	Myths and Fairy Stories. Thanksgiving Day and Christmas Stories. Poems	Myths and Fairy Stories. New Year and Washingt'n's Birthday Stories. Study of the Eskimo. Poems.	Myths and Fairy Stories. Decoration Day and Fourth of July Stories. Study of the Indian. Poems.
SECOND GRADE.	Myths and Fairy Stories. Thanksgiving Day and Christmas Stories. Poems.	Stories from the Odyssey. Story of Agoonack, from "Seven Little Sisters." New Year and Washingt'n's Birthday Stories. Poems.	Myths of Hiawatha. Decoration Day and Fourth of July Stories. Poems.
THIRD GRADE.	Stories of Inventions and Inventors. Reading of "Scudder's Fables and Folk Stories." Poems.	Early History of Chicago. Reading of "Little Folks of Other Lands," "Seven Little Sisters" and "Each and All." Poems.	Stories from Norse Mythology. Reading of "Robinson Crusoe." Poems.
FOURTH GRADE.	The Pilgrims and Puritans. Reading of Mara Pratt's American Hist'y Stories, Vol. 1, and Ruskin's King of the Golden River. Poems.	Other Pioneer Stories. Reading of Hawth'ne's Wonder Book and Tanglewood Tales. Poems.	Reading of De Garmo's Tales of Troy and "Swiss Family Robinson." Poems.
FIFTH GRADE.	Follow the Geography of North and South America by the study of Pre-Columbian History and Discovery and Exploration. Reading of Litchfield's The Nine Worlds and Poems.	Study of French discovery and exploration. History of Chicago. Reading of Longfellow's Hiawatha and "The Stories Mother Nature Told Her Children."	English Discovery and Exploration. Reading of Kingsley's Greek-Hero Stories, or "The Water Babies," or Baldwin's Stories of the Golden Age.
SIXTH GRADE.	Colonial History: Virginia, New England, New York. Reading of Longfellow's Miles Standish, Irving's Rip Van Winkle and Sleepy Hollow.	Colonial History, continued. Following the Geography of Asia, simple lessons on the History of China, India and Persia. Reading of "Ten Boys on the Road from Long Ago to Now," and A Hunting of the Deer (Warner).	The French and Indian War. Reading of Longfellow's Evangeline and Church's Stories from the Iliad. Poems.
SEVENTH GRADE.	The Revolutionary War. In connection with the Geography of Africa, simple lessons on the History of Egypt. Reading of Hawthorne's Tales of the White Hills and Church's Stories from Herodotus (selections).	The Revolutionary War, continued. The Critical Period. Study of Chaldæa and Assyria. Reading of Rogozin's Chaldæa (selections), Burrough's Birds and Bees, and Enoch Arden. Poems.	The Growth and Development of the Union to the Civil War. Simple lessons on the Middle Ages. Reading of Chaucer's Stories, Scott's Lady of the Lake, Lowell's Vision of Sir Launfal.
EIGHTH GRADE.	Review of the Growth and Development of the Union to the Civil War. Reading of 'Ulysses among the Phœnicians," Whittier's Among the Hills and other poems. Eyes and Other Papers.	The Civil War. Since 1865. Brief studies in the History of Greece and Rome. Reading of Plutarch's Lives (selections), Curtis' Prue and I, and Burrough's Sharp	Civics. Reading of Lowell's Poems. Selections.

ART-PROFESSIONAL TRAINING CLASS.

	FIRST TERM.	SECOND TERM.	THIRD TERM.
MODELING.	Botany—Fruits; vegetables; seeds; twigs, leaves, flowers. Zoology—Animals; birds; insects; nests; eggs; cocoons; bones. Mineralogy—Minerals. Geography—Forms of land. Conchology—Shells.	Form—Geometrical forms following the natural forms; cutting tablets. Geography—Forms of land and continents in sand.	History—From cast of historical ornament. Design—From original designs. Geography—Continents in putty.
PAINTING.	Botany—Fruits; vegetables; seeds; twigs, leaves, flowers and parts. Zoology—Animals; birds; insects; nests; cocoons; bones; muscle; enlarged parts of the same.	History—Egyptian and Grecian ornament. Design—Conventionalizing natural forms for border. Mineralogy—Minerals. Geology—Fossils. Conchology—Shells. Geography—Maps showing structure.	Botany—Germinating of seeds, flowers, trees, twigs and leaves. Geography—Outdoor sketching in color. Maps—Showing structure of continents and sections; political divisions.
DRAWING WITH PENCIL.	Physics—Apparatus used in science lessons; memory drawings of the same. Geography—Outdoor sketching on field excursions; all forms of land. Memory drawing of objects and places seen. Perspective—Converging lines.	Physics—Apparatus used in experiments; memory drawings of the same. Perspective—Linear and aerial; Interiors, Light and Shade. Geography—Continents showing structure. Literature—Illustrating stories.	Literature—Illustrating stories. History—Casts of historical ornament. Geography—Outdoor sketching; continents showing structure; political divisions. Platting—Ground plans of buildings and tracts of land.
RAPID SKETCHING ON BLACKBOARD.	Literature—Illustrating stories rapidly before the child. Geography—All forms of land, and objects seen on field excursions. Continents of North and South America, showing structure. Memory drawing of objects and places seen.	Literature—Illustrating stories. History—Parts of continents showing structure, also localities. Geography—Chalk modeling of all the continents. Perspective—Linear and aerial. Physics—Apparatus, also memory drawings of the same.	Literature—Illustrating stories. History—Localities pictured. Geography—Review of all continents, showing structure; political divisions.
CHALK MODELING.			
INVENTION. ORNAMENTAL DESIGN.	Science—Apparatus to be used in experiments. Working drawings made under the direction of Mr. Kenyon in the Sloyd rooms. Design—Conventionalizing natural forms.	Science—Apparatus to be used in experiments. Design—Principles of conventionalizing. Beginning of ornamental border from natural forms.	Science—Apparatus to be used in experiments. Design—Original border from natural forms.

ART-PRACTICE SCHOOL.

	MODELING.	PAINTING.	DRAWING.
FIRST GRADE.	BOTANY—Fruits; vegetables; seeds; twigs, leaves, flowers. ZOÖLOGY—Animals; birds; insects; nests; eggs; cocoons. FORM—Sphere; cube; cylinder; square prism.	BOTANY—Fruits, vegetables, seeds; twigs, leaves, flowers. ZOÖLOGY—Animals; birds; nests; eggs; cocoons; insects. PHYSICS—Flame; spectrum. DESIGN—Original arrangement of flowers for decorative design.	LITERATURE—Illustrating stories. HISTORY—Illustrating stories told. GEOGRAPHY—Places and forms of land seen. SCIENCE—Apparatus used in their experiments. Memory drawings.
SECOND GRADE.	BOTANY—Fruits; vegetables; seeds; twigs, leaves, flowers. ZOÖLOGY—Animals; birds; nests; eggs; insects; cocoons. FORM—Sphere; cube; cylinder; square prism; cone; ellipsoid; ovoid.	BOTANY—Fruits; vegetables; seeds; twigs, leaves, flowers, plants. ZOÖLOGY—Animals; birds; nests; eggs; insects; cocoons. GEOLOGY—Fossils. MINERALOGY—Minerals. PHYSICS—Flame; spectrum. DESIGN—Original arrangement of flowers.	LITERATURE—Illustrating stories. HISTORY—Illustrating stories. GEOGRAPHY—Places and forms of land seen. SCIENCE—Apparatus used in their experiments. Memory drawings.
THIRD GRADE.	BOTANY—Fruits; vegetables; seeds; twigs, leaves, flowers, nuts. ZOÖLOGY—Animals; birds; nests; eggs; insects; cocoons. MINERALOGY—Minerals. GEOLOGY—Fossils. GEOGRAPHY—Forms of land in sand. FORM—Square pyramid; tri-prism.	BOTANY—Fruits; vegetables; seeds; twigs, flowers, plants; nuts. ZOÖLOGY—Animals; birds; nests; eggs; insects; cocoons. GEOLOGY—Fossils; coral. MINERALOGY—Minerals. PHYSICS—Flame, spectrum. DESIGN—Original arrangement of flowers. GEOGRAPHY—Sketching out of doors.	LITERATURE—Illustrating stories. HISTORY—Illustrating stories. GEOGRAPHY—Forms of land. PHYSICS—Apparatus used. BOTANY—Twigs, leaves, trees. ZOÖLOGY—Birds; insects. Teach definite measurements and relative proportions. Memory drawings.
FOURTH GRADE.	BOTANY—Fruits; vegetables; seeds; nuts; twigs, leaves, flowers. ZOÖLOGY—Animals; birds; nests; insects; coral. MINERALOGY—Minerals. GEOLOGY—Fossils. CONCHOLOGY—Shells. GEOGRAPHY—Forms of land in sand.	BOTANY—Fruits; vegetables; seeds; nuts; plants; twigs, leaves, flowers. ZOÖLOGY—Bones; muscle; birds; insects. GEOLOGY—Fossils; coral. MINERALOGY—Minerals; stones. PHYSICS—Flame; spectrum. DESIGN—Conventionalized natural forms. GEOGRAPHY—Outdoor sketching. CONCHOLOGY—Shells.	LITERATURE—Illustrating stories. HISTORY—Pictures of localities and things. GEOGRAPHY—Forms of land. PHYSICS—Apparatus used. BOTANY—Enlarged parts of flowers and seeds. ZOÖLOGY—Enlarged parts of insects, etc. MINERALOGY—Minerals; stones. Teach definite measurements and relative proportions. Memory drawings.

ART PRACTICE SCHOOL.—Continued.

	MODELING.	PAINTING.	DRAWING.
FIFTH GRADE.	BOTANY—Fruits; seeds; nuts; vegetables; leaves. MINERALOGY—Minerals. GEOLOGY—Bones. ZOÖLOGY—Fossils. GEOGRAPHY—Forms of land and continents, in sand.	BOTANY—Fruits; seeds; nuts; vegetables; twigs, leaves, flowers, plants; buds with sections enlarged. ZOÖLOGY—Bones; muscle; birds; insects. GEOLOGY—Fossils; coral. MINERALOGY—Minerals; stones. PHYSICS—Flame; spectrum. CONCHOLOGY—Shells. DESIGN—Conventionalized natural forms. GEOGRAPHY—Outdoor sketching.	LITERATURE—Illustrating stories. HISTORY—Picturing of places and things. GEOGRAPHY—Structure of North and South America. PHYSICS—Apparatus used in experiments. BOTANY—Enlarged parts of flowers and plants. ZOÖLOGY—Insects and parts enlarged. MINERALOGY—Minerals; stones. DESIGN—Conventionalizing of natural forms. Memory drawings. Relative proportions; definite measurements.
SIXTH GRADE.	BOTANY—Fruits; seeds; nuts; vegetables; leaves. MINERALOGY—Minerals. GEOLOGY—Fossils. ZOÖLOGY—Bones. GEOGRAPHY—Forms of land and continents, in sand.	BOTANY—Fruits; seeds; nuts; vegetables; plants, leaves, flowers; trees, twigs, buds with sections enlarged. ZOÖLOGY—Bones; muscle; birds; insects. GEOLOGY—Fossils; coral. MINERALOGY—Minerals; stones. PHYSICS—Flame; spectrum. DESIGN—Conventionalized natural forms. GEOGRAPHY—Outdoor sketching; maps.	LITERATURE—Illustrating stories. HISTORY—Picturing of places and things. GEOGRAPHY—Structure of North and South America. PHYSICS—Apparatus used in experiments. BOTANY—Parts of flowers and plants enlarged. ZOÖLOGY—Insects and parts enlarged. DESIGN—Conventionalized natural forms for border. Memory drawings. PERSPECTIVE—Converging lines.
SEVENTH GRADE.	BOTANY—Fruits; seeds; nuts; vegetables; leaves. MINERALOGY—Minerals. GEOLOGY—Fossils. GEOGRAPHY—Continents of North and South America, in sand; also Eurasia, Africa and Australia; political divisions of same.	BOTANY—Fruits; seeds; vegetables; plants, leaves, flowers; trees, twigs, buds with sections enlarged. ZOÖLOGY—Bones; muscle; insects. GEOLOGY—Fossils; coral. MINERALOGY—Minerals; stones. PHYSICS—Spectrum. HISTORY—Ornament, Egyptian. DESIGN—Conventionalized natural forms. GEOGRAPHY—Outdoor sketching; maps.	LITERATURE—Illustrating stories. HISTORY—Egyptian. GEOGRAPHY—Structure of North and South America, Eurasia, Africa and Australia; also sections. PHYSICS—Apparatus used in experiments. BOTANY—Parts of flowers and plants enlarged. ZOÖLOGY—Insects and parts enlarged. DESIGN—Conventionalizing of natural forms for border. Memory drawings. PERSPECTIVE—Converging lines; linear perspective.
EIGHTH GRADE.	BOTANY—Fruits; seeds; vegetables; leaves. GEOGRAPHY—In sand, all the continents and sections; political divisions.	BOTANY—Fruits; seeds; vegetables; plants, leaves, flowers; trees, twigs, buds with sections enlarged. ZOÖLOGY—Bones; muscle; insects. GEOLOGY—Fossils; coral. PHYSICS—Spectrum. HISTORY—Greek ornament. DESIGN—Conventionalizing of natural forms for border. GEOGRAPHY—Outdoor sketching; maps—showing construction of land.	LITERATURE—Illustrating stories. HISTORY—Greek ornament. GEOGRAPHY—Structure of all the continents; also political divisions and sections. PHYSICS—Apparatus used in experiments. Memory drawings. BOTANY—Parts of flowers and plants enlarged. ZOÖLOGY—Insects and parts enlarged. DESIGN—Conventionalizing of forms for border. PERSPECTIVE—Linear and aerial.

MANUAL TRAINING—PROFESSIONAL TRAINING CLASS.

Manual training in pasteboard, wood sloyd and apparatus construction, is to prepare teachers (1) to give regular courses in pasteboard and wood sloyd; (2) to train pupils to make apparatus needed in science and other teaching; (3) to be able to skillfully use any method of teaching and training that demands hand-work; (4) to cultivate a great love and profound respect for manual labor.

PURPOSES OF MANUAL TRAINING.

1. The main purpose of manual training is to develop logical power by practical sequences of construction that require an accurate knowledge of the exact relations of parts to each other, and each part to the whole.

2. Manual training develops the imagination by demanding the realization of distinct concepts.

3. It trains the will in the steady persistence necessary to completely express a concept.

4. Exercises in educative manual training are the most practical lessons in form and number.

5. The ethical or altruistic motive is cultivated by making each model of direct practical use, in the school, in the home and otherwise.

6. Love and respect for manual labor is developed by the constant and sustained emotion that the making and the maker are of direct and immediate use to mankind.

7. Habits of order, exactness, cleanliness and neatness are formed by educative handwork.

8. Educative sloyd is the best possible physical training. It is found to be an excellent means of remedying nervousness and balancing the overstrain of purely intellectual work.

9. Sloyd is an indispensable foundation and preparation for art studies.

The members of the Professional Training Class take the course herewith given for the Practice School.

MANUAL TRAINING—FOR THE PRACTICE SCHOOL.

GRADE.	FIRST TERM.		SECOND TERM.		THIRD TERM.	
	CARDBOARD SLOYD:	PHYSICS APPARATUS:	CARDBOARD SLOYD:	PHYSICS APPARATUS:	CARDBOARD SLOYD:	PHYSICS APPARATUS:
FIRST.	Knife game. Name card. Thread winder. Circle maker.	Book mark. Seed tray.	Magnetic needle stand (wire). Seed envelope, No. 1. Desk-cloth holder. Lever and block.	Bound book, No. 1. Match strike. Match box (by stenc'l).	Work envelope. Tri-button tray. Sugar tray.	Soil sieve.
SECOND.	Rule game. Thread winder. Circle maker.	Book mark. Cube. Seed tray. Bound book, No. 1.	Magnetic needle stand (wood). Seed envelope, No. 2. Lever and block.	Match strike, No. 2. Work envelope, No. 2. Portfolio, No. 1.	Triple screen.	Match box, No. 2. Bound book, No. 2. Cube.	Soil sieve.
THIRD.	Rule game. Book mark. Seed envelope.	Match box, No. 1. Work envelope, No. 2.	Magnetette needle stand (wood). Seed envelope, No. 2. Mineral tray. Lever and block.	Match stand. Portfolio, No. 1. Hex-tray.	Mineral fork. Triple screen.	Portfolio, No. 2. Tri-tray (oblique). Bound book, No. 2.	Soil sieve.
FOURTH.	Book mark. Seed envelope. Work envelope.	Match safe, No. 2. Tri-tray (oblique).	Shadow stick. Magnetette needle stand. Seed envelope, No. 2. Mineral tray. Lever and block.	Lotus tray.	Mineral fork. Triple screen. Base for lens and screen.	Bound book, No. 4.	Base for lens and screen. Soil sieve.
	WOOD SLOYD:		WOOD SLOYD:		WOOD SLOYD:	
FIFTH.	Match strike.	Sandpaper block. Molding tool.	Shadow stick. Needle stand. Seed envelope, No. 2. Mineral tray. Lever and block.	Thread winder. Paper knife.	Mineral fork. Reflector stand.	Easel. Letter opener.	Screen. Soil sieve.
SIXTH.	Match safe. Pen rest.		Shadow stick. Needle stand. Seed envelope, No. 2. Mineral tray. Expander.	Trellis. Foot rule.	Pendulum stand (1st part). Mineral fork. Reflector stand.	Bulletin board. Pointer.	Lens holder. Climatometer.
SEV'TH.	Pin bowl. Blackboard ruler.		Shadow stick. Needle stand. Expander. Bi-metal conductor.	American axe-shaft. Picture frame.	Pendulum stand (2d part). Mineral fork. Reflector stand.	Coat hooks.	Climatometer. Butterfly net.
EIGHTH.	Drawing board. Book stall.		Shadow stick. Needle stand. Expander. Bi-metal conductor.	Scoop. Knife box.	Pendulum stand (3d part). Mineral fork. Reflector stand.	Bread board (curved). Paper knife, No. 2 (carved). Pupil's own device.	Climatometer. Butterfly net.

PHYSICAL TRAINING—EXPLANATORY.

Professional Training Class.

The design of the work of this department is to better fit all participants in it to lead a life of usefulness to their fellow-beings.

It is not designed merely for personal improvement and recreation, but with reference to the future work of the teacher.

Through its influence the teacher shall attain that consciousness of power which inspires courage to do right and which makes possible a quick resolution to act when exigencies must be suited.

Health and strength are regarded as the basis for intellectual upbuilding.

The preparatory work embraces the study of rules of conduct of a school, of order, correct standing and sitting habits, of proper carriage and bearing of pupils in and out of school.

This study, reviewing the best methods for securing promptness, aptness of person, or class, in obeying commands, orderly arrangement and dismissal of classes, energetic and graceful execution of desirable movements, etc., is supplemented by a review of the laws governing freedom of motion; the best methods for school-room ventilation, dress, habits.

The numerous school-house committees, selected with a view to engage all members of the school in their turn in house-keeping duties, are governed in part by the rules which result in adoption after earnest discussion.

In the first term of the school year questions are selected for discussion on part of the teachers and pupils that have a direct bearing on school and health habits, the maintenance of mental and physical health under varying conditions.

The Theory of Gymnastics is defined in accord with the best German writers on Educational Gymnastics.

The pupil teacher, as is readily seen, should be able at the close of the school year to give a fair interpretation of the work done in this department, either in the school-room, yard, or hall, independently of any manual.

The teaching of groups in this work (calisthenics) is commenced immediately upon the opening of school by members of the Prof. Training Class of the previous year, of whom a sufficient number for all groups have heretofore attended.

The plan of work in detail for the entire school-year for the Prof. Training Class, outlined in part only in the following pages, is as follows:

Firstly, illustrations are given in the relation of gymnastic work to other forms of expression; suggestions are made on incidental themes, embracing information on physical culture. Information as regards methods and rules to be observed with regard to gymnastic exercises, time for exercises, order of exercises (progression), in and out-door work and play, ventilation in halls, corridors, rooms, is regularly imparted.

All work centering in the work of the Practice School, the same is arranged to suit the group work outlined in another part of this report. In order to secure its correct adaptation to the various grades of the school at the beginning and throughout the first term of the year, charts, giving the correct outline of the work for each grade, are posted for the guidance of the pupil teachers. One such chart is posted for each grade per month. The work outlined in these charts, and practiced in divisions of pupil-teachers throughout the regular gymnastic periods, is elementary and designed to fully acquaint the teachers with the resp. nomenclature. The work throughout this term is copied, memorized and given during the practice-hour. Stress is laid upon its correct interpretation and execution. It is criticised according to a formula handed the critic-teachers, who also have a regular course in calisthenic work throughout the months of September and October, besides participating in the work of the so-called 'Volunteer Classes.' Lack of controlling power in this work, requiring in the beginning studious effort on the part of the pupil-teacher, necessitates a supplementary course on account of inefficient work. The critic teacher making such report fills such pupil-teacher's place with some other member of the training class.

Pupil-teachers cannot go beyond the work outlined in the charts, in which a careful progression is observed.

The general supervision, criticism and final direction is referred to the head of this department, subject to the discussion and revision of the whole corps of teachers.

The following branches, to which reference is made in the other departments of the school, conjointly with the gymnastic work proper, serve to convince the pupil-teacher of the importance of physical education and furnish an adequate idea of the resposibilities entailed:

Anthropology, anatomy and physiology, hygiene—personal and public health; pedagogies, with special reference to such forms of gymnastics, arranged to meet an educational purpose and adaptable to schools to which teachers may be called; influence of mind on body, etc., voice culture, music, Delsarte system of expression, anthropometry; modeling, drawing; history of gymnastics.

The regular teachers are enjoined whenever a necessity appears for it, to arouse their pupils by a short interval of calisthenic exercises. During each school session 10 15 minutes (the minimum) is devoted to these exercises. The different grades, receiving twice per week 30-40 minutes gymnastic exercises in the gymnasium under direction of the special teacher are sufficiently prepared for the work designed in the monthly charts for the guidance also of the teachers. The work of each chart contains an outline for the current month—one chapter of work per week. In the first term the group leader, selected for gymnastic work, leads throughout one whole month, frequent changes of leaders not being deemed advisable at this stage of the work. The group leaders form a special class for preparatory instruction.

The term closes with a criticism of the papers called for in which the various topics discussed throughout the same are reviewed.

These papers invariably prove that the self-governing form of the school already to an extent influenced opinions that prevailed before attempts to utilize the many suggestions made were seriously considered. To insure success in directing exercises, for inst.

during practice-teaching, when six or eight groups would be in close proximity to each other, or when exercising the large volunteer classes, that would meet for personal improvement after school-hours, would always entail a degree of governing power, that would make the pupil-teacher quick to substitute remedial means for recognized failures. Those who could not recognize their weaknesses, were invariably helped along by others taking part in the work.

The tabulations of the *second* term, which are also copied, contain the progression in positions and changes of position that invariably precede other work; they furthermore contain the indications only of the work proper the teachers themselves are now required to adapt to some form of combination of exercises (in the outline of progression) required. In this term *all* pupil-teachers in a group teach gymnastics in turn, beginning with group leader, the assistants of a group taking their turn in the following week. Work of the preceding day should not be repeated in the same form the following day.

Criticisms in all work, as correctness of commands in good English, arranging and dismissing classes, order, choice and execution of exercises, bearing of pupils and teacher, massing and marching, are freely given. Criticisms of pupil-teachers in command are also indulged in by all members of a class present. In this manner the best possible use of the time of the regular school periods is made.

A system of measurements adapted to the several grades, partially begun last year, is continued at present under the most unfavorable conditions. Not until the gymnasium, which at this writing seems to be an assured fact, stands well equipped, can satisfactory results be reached in this work.

In addition to these measurements other tests considering strength, agility, etc., are made at the close of the school-year in the week preceding "field-day."

The last term is devoted to special work in the line of progression, to exercises and drills with hand apparatus, light gymnastics, to order gymnastics (tactics) for school discipline in and out-doors, to out-door gymnastics. Discussions and criticisms of all work, different methods are held, and some time is devoted to the games written by students, their discussion, etc. Medical gymnastics, emergencies (first aid) are reviewed at the close of the term.

Those capable of teaching sections and divisions are now entrusted with classes consisting of one or more grades. This work done in the gymnasium (or Assembly Hall) is always criticised by one or more of the advanced pupil-teachers. Such written criticisms are given the special teacher, who compares the same with his own for discussion with the pupil-teachers, whereupon the pupil-teacher is required to write out a model-lesson on light gymnastics for the school library.

Primary grades have about two hours per week for regular exercises; grammar grades the same, with the exception of those pupils who attend the grammar volunteer classes after school, who, with the members of the Training Class, attending special Volunteer classes, have about five hours per week for gymnastic instruction, exclusive of the work of practice-teaching.

PHYSICAL TRAINING—PRACTICE SCHOOL.

First Grade—First Term.

ORDER EXERCISES.

Rising and Sitting Exercises—Fundamental Position. Resting Position. Pos. 'Rest'.—Alignments: ranging according to size; the front rank, flank rank.—Quarter facings.—Stepping, (forw., backw., sidew., with hand-clapping, first, last movement).—Simple connections (linking) in front and flank ranks.—Marching 'on place'.—Distancing, arm's length, in flank ranks.

FIRST MOVEMENT EXERCISES—Preparatory.

Positions executed to *command.*—Head: bending, turning.—Shoulders: raising, moving.—Arms: raising, (forw., upw., sidew.); hands, grasped backw.; arms, bent to thrust; folded (forw., backw.); hands on (under) shoulders; on hips, chest, locked overhead, behind head, backw., forw., (starting positions). Trunk: bending, (forw., backw., sidew.); turning.—Legs: stepping motions (forw., backw., sidew.); raising, bending.—Feet: rising heels, toes.—Seat exercises: leaning backw., hands behind head; sitting erect.

Change of Positions—Moving head, trunk, shoulders, arms, legs, feet, from one position to another.

Elementary Exercises:—(simple exercises, executed with one member, or part of one member of the body, as one leg, one arm (l. r., in rhythm), two counts for each movement). Head: bending, (forw., backw., sidew.); turning. Arms: raising, placing, straightening, thrusting —Trunk: bending, (forw., backw., sidew.); turning. Legs: knee-bending and raising; step, ½-stride pos.., (forw., backw., sidew.)—Feet, alternate raising of heels and toes.

First Grade—Second Term.

See foregoing exercises. Add:

Rising and sitting ex. on place, (turning seats). Formation of a line of ranks by stepping forw. (front rank), sidew. (flank rank), and aligning l., r.—Formation of a line of ranks by alternate facings.—Open class order, stepping forw., (sidew.), each pupil of a rank a given number of steps.—Marching on place in connection with quarter-facings.—Marching on place, marking given steps of a number, by stamping, clapping hands, etc.

FIRST MOVEMENT EXERCISES.

See foregoing exercises. Add:
Head: rolling, bowing.—Shoulders; shrugging.—Arms: starting pos. as ex. (double).—Trunk: bending, with hands on shoulders, or behind head.—Legs: running, with arms bent to thrust.—Feet: turning on the balls.
Breathing ex., with arm raising and lowering, (forw., sidew.)

COMBINATIONS.

Elementary exercises executed as combinations of simple movements, consecutively executed, and as combinations of double movements consecutively executed, and as combinations of simple movements, simultaneously executed.
(Double exercises are executed with two like members of the body, as both arms, hands, legs, feet.)

FIRST GRADE.—THIRD TERM.

See foregoing exercises. Add:
Rising and sitting ex., l. and r.—Marching of flank ranks, r. angle.—Formation of ranks by consecutive facings of a given number of pupils upon reaching angle—Alignments of a column.—Marching sidew. of files in consecutive and simultaneous order.—Alignment of files and flank ranks in open order.—Stepping forw., backw., sidew., eyes r., (l), a given number of steps—Running, 'circuit.'

FREE MOVEMENT EXERCISES.

See foregoing exercises. Add:
Shoulders: simultaneously raising, lowering (arm positions).—Arms: raising, sidew. l., r., arm circle overhead; turning locked hands while extending arms in diff. directions; bending, hands grasped forw., backw.—Hands. swinging up and down, sidew., in diff. positions of the arms.—Trunk: bending forw with hollow back (arm pos.).—Legs: knee-bending on tip-toe.
Breathing ex.: quick, hands stemmed firmly against the hips (sides).
Plays.

COMBINATIONS.

Combination of elementary exercises.—Double movements, simultaneously executed. Simple movements, intersected. Double movements, intersected. Simple exercises of more than two motions.

SECOND GRADE.—FIRST TERM.

See foregoing exercises. Add:
Alignments—dressing, covering—Marching forw., backw., a given number of steps.—Formation of the circle from the front rank.—Open and close circle, (distancing).—Formation of a line of ranks by taking arm positions, etc., (a given number in consecutive order). Distancing obliquely.

FREE MOVEMENT EXERCISES.—PREPARATORY.

See foregoing exercises. Add:
Positions.—Head: bowing,—Shoulders and arms, (hands on shoulders); raise elbows. move forw., backw.; straightening, thrusting, moving, from starting pos.—Trunk: bowing.—Legs: raising, bending, r. angle; ½ stride pos. forw., backw., sidew.—Feet: turning,—Seat exercises: arm and head movements.
Changes of positions.—Trunk-bending in ½ stride pos., forw., backw.

COMBINATIONS.

Elementary exercises:—Simple, executed l., r., and alternately l. and r.
Elementary exercises:—Double, executed with two like members of the body, (both arms, feet, legs.)

SECOND GRADE.—SECOND TERM.

See foregoing exercises. Add:
Rising and sitting in connection with marching from pl. (class formation for marching order, fire-drill). Formation of a line of ranks by successive connections of a number, linking.—Open class-order by stepping forw., sidew., each pupil of a rank a given number of steps.—Close class-order, opp. directions.—Marching on place in connection with facings, and hand-clapping.

FREE MOVEMENT EXERCISES.

See foregoing exercises. Add:
Head: rolling, in half-stride pos.—Trunk: rocking, forw., backw., and sidew., l. and r.—Legs: turning feet to half-stride pos. sidew., rising on tip-toe; turning on heels in half-stride pos. sidew.—Running, raising heels backw.—Feet: close-stand pos.
Breathing exercises with chest percussion.
Plays.

COMBINATIONS.

Elementary exercises are executed as combinations of simple movements, consecutively executed; as combinations of double movements, consecutively executed; as combinations of simple movements, consecutively executed.

SECOND GRADE.—THIRD TERM.

See foregoing exercises. Add:
Facings behind desks.—Marching of the flank rank, speaking aloud a certain number of a given number of steps.—Marching on tip-toe.—Simple step, short step, quick step.—Counting in ranks in open order.—Running, furlong.—Halting.

FREE MOVEMENT EXERCISES.

See foregoing exercises. Add:
Arms: turning, (forw., backw., sidew., l., r., outward, inward), in dif. positions, (forw., upw., sidew., downw.) Hands: close, open, rub, in diff. pos., arms flexed, extended. —Trunk: bending, downward.—Legs: turning on heels, toes, in half-stride pos. forw., l., r., kneeling. Feet: close, part.
Breathing ex.: raise arms sidew., inhale; lower backw., exhale.
Plays.

COMBINATIONS.

Combinations of elementary exercises:—Double movements, simultaneously executed; simple movements, intersected; double, ditto; simple ex. of more than two motions.—Combinations.

THIRD GRADE—FIRST TERM.

See foregoing exercises. Add:
Alignments: dressing towards rank's center.—About-facings.—Marching sidew. of closed ranks. Marching forward of flank ranks. r. angle.—Marching to circle.—Formation of lines of ranks by stepping forw. and backward, alternately.—Formation of a column of ranks from a line of ranks by successive wheeling.—Formation of a column of ranks from a flank line in consecutive order, while on a line of march.—Connections.—Distancing: half, full distance, or a given number of steps.

FREE MOVEMENT EXERCISES.—PREPARATORY.

See foregoing exercises. Add:
Positions.—Head: rolling.—Shoulders and arms: arm circle overhead; swinging; striking from starting pos., (arms flexed); raising in two diff. directions simultaneously.—Trunk: bending in oblique directions.—Legs: swinging, turning, bending to acute angle; stride-pos. forw., buckw., sidew.—Feet: turning.—Seat and desk ex.: Trunk leaning, bending, (sidew., forw., backw).
Changes of pos.—Trunk turning, bending, in ½-stride pos. forw.

COMBINATIONS.

Elementary exercises:—Simple, executed l., r., and alternately. Simple and double, executed alternately.
Elementary exercises: Double, are executed with two members, or two parts of like members of the body, (both arms, both hands).—Arms: raising, swinging, flexing, extending.—Legs: bending, extending.

THIRD GRADE.—SECOND TERM.

See foregoing exercises. Add:
Rising and marching to 'class-order;' Order: 'in ranks.'—Formation of a line of ranks by counting.—Wheeling.—Distancing sidew. in a front rank by marching forw., linked order. Close order by closing intervals l., r., towards centre.—Marching on place in connection with about-facings.—Marching on place, facing on the first of a given number of steps.

FREE MOVEMENT EXERCISES.

See foregoing exercises. Add:
Head: pressing backw. against hands in pos.—Trunk: turn-bending forw.—Legs: turning, flexing backw.—Feet: rocking, striking heels, toes, together; stamping.—Legs and feet; rising on tiptoe, bending knees in ½-stride pos. sidew. Running, clapping hands on the first of a given number of steps.
Breathing ex. with head-bending backw.
Plays.

COMBINATIONS.

Exercises are executed as combinations of simple and double movements, simultaneously, and as combinations of double movements, consecutively, also as combination of movements executed in consecution (intersected).

THIRD GRADE.—THIRD TERM.

See foregoing exercises. Add:

Hang-and stem-exercises between desks.—Formation of curved lines (½-circle, circle in front and flank, by alternate forming l. and r.—Counter-marching of flank ranks; oblique marching.—Counting off in files in open order.—Marching ex. of a column, (linked order); change step, etc.—Running, halting.—Column close-order.

FREE MOVEMENT EXERCISES.

See foregoing exercises. Add:

Shoulder: circling.—Arms: flinging (from hands on chest, or on sh.); circling sidew.—Forearms: striking.—Hands: circling.—Trunk: turn-bending backw.—Legs: raising thighs, knees, forw., upw.; stepping-motions with opp. knee bent; hopping-ex. on both feet; running on place, swinging legs forw.—Seat and desk exercises; oblique alignments l. r., (arm movement, writing ex.)

Breathing ex.: arm circle overhead, during a given number of counts.

Plays.

COMBINATIONS.

Double, simultaneously executed; simple and double, of more than two motions, executed, l., r., both, outward, inward.

FOURTH GRADE.—FIRST TERM.

See foregoing exercises. Add:

Alignments.—Counting off.- Wheeling in successive and simultaneous order, (quarter, half circles.)—Transformations of a line of flank ranks to a column of front ranks, by forming l. (r.) in the ranks (following).—Marching forw. of a column, r. angles.—Marching sidew. (alignment) in close-pos.—Formation of a column of two files from a line in flank running from place: Formation of a body of ranks (while on a line of march) by simultaneous quarter wheelings of two or more ranks at a given place.—Distancing a given number of paces, from a centre.

FREE MOVEMENT EXERCISES.

See foregoing exercises. Add:

Arms: placing in angular pos., bent upw., forw.; raising backw.—Trunk: turning and bending in stride-pos. sidew.—Legs and feet: stepping motions on tip-toe; twirling about (on balls of feet); rocking on tip-toe; running with knee-bending.

Breathing ex.: Hands on hips, bending head backw.

COMBINATIONS.

Elementary exercises: Simple, executed, l, r., and alternately. Simple and double, executed alternately.

FOURTH GRADE.—SECOND TERM.

See foregoing exercises. Add:

Marching forw. of a front line (of ranks) a given number of steps, and wheeling to a column in front.—Wheeling to open order.—Forming of front to flank, flank to front ranks, by forming next first or last, or behind l. or r. (following).—Formation of a column from a line in front, successive wheelings, passing line in front.—Counter-marching of a column.—Counter-marching, r. angle-marching of flank ranks of a column.—Formations of two columns marching in opp. directions, by successive wheelings of one or more ranks at a given place, in alternate order.—Uniting of columns to a colonnade.—Distancing outward, full distance, by forming, passing rear.—Circling in open order of odd or even files; same odd and even files simultaneously.

FREE GYMNASTICS.—LIGHT GYMNASTICS.

See preceding exercises. Add:

Arms: thrusting in connection with circling.—Facings, with arms crossed, hands grasped.—Dumb-bell ex.—Legs: balance movements; marching, flexing backw., raising knees.—Marching long distance. Jumping, running. Feet: rocking on tip-toe in step, ½-stride, stride-pos., sidew., forw.

Breathing exercises: Rise on tip-toe, bending arms, hands grasped backw., and inhale; straighten arms and lower heels, exhale.

Plays.

COMBINATIONS.

Simple exercises, simultaneously executed; double exercises, consecutively executed; double exercises, executed as consecution of movements.

FOURTH GRADE—THIRD TERM.

See preceding exercises. Add:

Marching in oblique directions from flank order, forw., backw.—First method forming, running.—First method forming, divided order, (from flank to front rank by forming alternately l., r.)

LIGHT GYMNASTICS.

Wand, Dumb-bell exercises, marching.—Pole exercises.—Skipping exercises.

EPERCISES.	FIELD EXERCISES.
Breathing exercise: deep breathing, running on place. Plays.	Running exercises. Games.

FIFTH GRADE—FIRST TERM.

See foregoing exercises. Add:

Alignment with a given point of a rank.—Counting off from l. to r., or r. to l.—Forming in flank ranks. Distancing in flank ranks, forw., backw., a given number of steps.—Wheeling of flank ranks, linked order.—Transformation of a column of ranks in flank to a line in front.—Forming l., r., in front ranks, passing rear.—Distancing outward a given number of steps.—Simultaneous change of places (pairs).—Single marching in squares (open order).

FREE GYMNASTICS.

See foregoing exercises. Add:

Arms: circling, forw., backw.; raising upw. in pos.,sidew., forw.; raising, in connection with turning.—Trunk: bending in obl. directions.—Legs and feet: alternate knee-bending in half-stride pos.; oblique stepping motions; marching, rocking on tip-toes; hopping on and from place; running, raising knees forw.
Breathing exercises: straighten arms upw., bending trunk backw., inhale.

COMBINATIONS.

Elementary Exercises: simple, exec. l. and r., alternately, and l., r.; simple, simultaneously executed; simple and double, alternately executed.

FIFTH GRADE—SECOND TERM.

See preceding exercises. Add:

Formation of a column of flank ranks from a flank line by angular marching of ranks.—Marching forw., backw., a given number of steps and wheeling of flank ranks.—Angular marching of flank ranks to lines, and counter-marching of ranks in a line.—Distancing in a front rank by marching forw. l., r., or from centre.—Forming l., r., in front ranks, by passing front.—Forming in flank ranks, to the rear, by passing l., r.—Forming to open order in flank ranks, in front or rear, by passing l., r.—Repetition of formations, first method, running.—Forming in connections with facings.

FREE AND LIGHT GYMNASTICS.

See preceding exercises. Add:

Swinging, hurling, thrusting, throwing of sacks, balls. Antagonistics: pulling, pushing, turning, twisting, twirling, wrenching (hand apparatus).—Dumb-bell ex.—Change-step, schottische; step ex. in connection with ex.: three-beat step; turn-trunk-step; turn-step; fencing-step, close-step.
Breathing ex.: head backw., arms upw., inhale; lower forw. slowly, exhale.
Plays.

COMBINATIONS.

Double exercises, executed as consecution of movements; double exercises, simultaneously executed: simple and double movements of more than two movements (l. r., both.)

FIFTH GRADE—THIRD TERM.

See preceding exercises. Add:

Forming in front. flank ranks, in connection with distancing.—Second method of forming (obliquing).—Forming in front ranks, passing front and rear alternately. Same in flank ranks, passing l. and r. alternately.—Forming next first or last of flank ranks, divided order (l. and r. alternately, following, from flank to front rank).

EXERCISES.	FIELD EXERCISES.
Sack-swinging, tossing, in open class order.—Preparatory swimming ex.—Wand and dumb-bell ex., marching. Breathing ex.: inhale, marching on place 10-20 steps. Plays.	Circuit-racing.—Long wand ex. Antagonistics. Games.

SIXTH GRADE—FIRST TERM.

See foregoing exercises. Add:

Counting off in conn. with stepping forw. to align.—Wheeling about l. or r. flank.—Forming in front l. or r., l. or r. by obliquing.—Stepping forw., backw., sidew., of even or odd files.—Forming forw., backw., l. or r., to open order, full distance, from a line in front or flank in close order, and closing.—Counter-marching of ranks, files, in open order (skeleton drill).—Marching of two columns in opp. directions (crossing).—Marching of flank ranks in squares.

FREE AND LIGHT GYMNASTICS.

See foregoing exercises. Add:

Arms: circling, l., r., forw., backw., sidew., (mill).—Dumb-bell ex.—Trunk: circling.—Legs and feet: cross-stepping motions; squatting pos.; marching, swing-step forw., backw.; running on place in connection with facings.
Breathing ex.: Hands on chest and move arms sidew. slowly, inhaling.

COMBINATIONS.

Simple exercises, executed l. and r., alternately, and l., r.; simple exercises, simultaneously executed; simple and double exercises, alternately executed.

SIXTH GRADE—SECOND TERM.

See preceding exercises. Add:

Wheeling about a front rank's centre.—Forming in rear l., r., l. or r. of last, by obliquing. Repeat first method forming in ranks, running.—Simple wheelings, running.—Circling in files, ranks.

FREE AND LIGHT GYMNASTICS.

See preceding exercises. Add:

Measure-step, close-step, cross-close-step, knee-bend-step, backw. flexing-step, (same in conn. with leg extension); foot-rocking-step, trunk-rocking-step (forw., backw., sidew., l. or r.); marching, swinging legs forw. in semi-circle; balance-marching and hopping-step; schottische-step, waltz-step, basque-step.—Cross-step running, cross-hopping-step, change-hopping-step, change-triple-step, etc.—Free ex. while marching, galop-running.—Stooping pos. as balance-movements.—Spiral, or maze marching, hopping, running.
Breathing ex.: Arch arms overhead, bending backw., and inhale.
Plays.

COMBINATIONS.

Double exercises, executed as consecution of movements; double exercises, executed simultaneously; simple and double movement exercises of more than two motions—(l. r., both).

SIXTH GRADE—THIRD TERM.

See preceding exercises. Add:

First method forming, marching from place.—Second method forming, running on place.—Second method forming (obliquing), divided order.—Marching sidew. of front ranks, r. angles.—Counter and serpentine circling.—Counter-marching of files, facing opp. directions.—From a front rank, alternate forming—front, rear—to a flank rank (divided order).

EXERCISES.	FIELD EXERCISES.
Running, marching, (one, two, or more), under long swinging rope. Tactic exercises with song accompaniment. Support exercises with long wands. Iron dumb-bell exercises. Breathing exercises: sighing, hissing—exhaling. Plays.	Exercises on balance-boards.—Running exercises on the track.—Distance-marching, running. Throwing of balls, spears.—Hurdle running (2' 6").—Hop, skip and jump. Exercises with the heavy ropes (tug-of-war). Games.

SEVENTH GRADE—FIRST TERM.

See foregoing exercises. Add:

Formation of ranks by successive stepping backw. of a given number in connection with signal exercises and aligning.—Wheeling of a flank or front rank about any member of a rank.—Forming by circling.—Forming in front of flank ranks by passing l., r.—Oblique marching of a body of ranks.—Formation l., r., in front ranks, opp. flank beginning.—Formation in flank ranks, last member beginning.

FREE AND LIGHT GYMNASTICS.

See foregoing exercises. Add:

Arms: angular pos. sidew., forw., circling of shoulders, hands on same; angular pos. (arms bent) upw. forw., downw.—Wand exercises.—Trunk: bending in stride-pos. forw., sidew.—Legs: oblique stride-pos.; cross-stride (half) pos.—Feet: twirling l., r., from cross-step pos. forw. (¼ turn).—Running, swinging legs sidew.; skipping on place.
Breathing exercise: deep breathing.

COMBINATIONS.

Simple and double exercises, alternately executed; Simple and double exercises, simultaneously executed; Double exercises, executed as consecution of movements; Double exercises, simultaneously executed.

SEVENTH GRADE—SECOND TERM.

See preceding exercises. Add:
Formation of a line (in flank) by successive stepping sidew. of ranks, in conn. with ex.—Forming in flank ranks from place to first place by passing in front.—Same by passing rear; same l., r., in a front rank.—Forming l., r., in front ranks, passing front, opp. flank beginning.—Forming front or rear of flank ranks, opp. leader beginning.—Chain march; the loop; intertwining of two or more circles. Figure-marching (cross, star, etc.); forming in ranks of a figure; transformation of bodies.—Forming by obliquing, running.

FREE AND LIGHT GYMNASTICS

See preceding exercises. Add:
Group ex. with dumb-bells, clubs.—Antagonistics, with and without apparatus.—Support ex.; raising, balancing, carrying.—Close-step with thigh and leg flexions and extensions.—Ex. in prone-support, or prone pos.—Free gymnastics, while marching, running.—Ex. in hopping; double-change-step, simple change-hopping-step, double-change-hopping-step.—Bounding-step (running). Leg: circling. Hopping ex., under long rope.
Breathing ex.: arch l., then r., arm overhead, bending sidew. in opp. directions, in haling.
Plays.

COMBINATIONS.

Double exercises, simultaneously executed; Simultaneously executed exercises of more than two motions.

SEVENTH GRADE—THIRD TERM.

See preceding exercises. Add:
Different methods forming, marching from place.—Wheeling of front, flank ranks in connection with marching sidew. (forw., backw.) r. angles.—Marching sidew., l., r., of front ranks, in connection with facings—Forming in front ranks, passing front and rear, alternately, opp. flank beginning.—Forming in flank ranks, passing l. and r., alternately, opp. leader beginning.—Figure-marching; star-wheel, fan; double chain; double circling in triple groups.

EXERCISES.	FIELD EXERCISES.
Complicated group exercises.—Memory exercises.—Support ex. (group ex.) with short wands.—Club and dumb-bell ex.—Similar, dissimilar group ex., with song accompaniment. Breathing ex.: deep breathing, whistle, exhaling. Plays.	Exercise on the balancing beam and board—Skipping as class ex., in connection with facings. Time-marching and running; track ex.—Stick twirling, stick wrestling.—Support ex. (pyramidal). Hurdle running (3').—Throwing light javelin.—Putting light stone.—Pole vaulting. Games.

EIGHTH GRADE—FIRST TERM.

See preceding exercises. Add:
Combinations of wheeling and forming in front and flank ranks (first method). Combinations of forming, facings and wheelings. Combinations of forming, (second method; obliquing), and wheeling.—Combinations of forming by circling and wheeling about a given person.—Combinations of marching of flank ranks, in squares, (r. angle). or counter, and wheeling about first or last member of rank—File drill.

FREE AND LIGHT GYMNASTICS—COMPLICATED EXERCISES.

See foregoing exercises. Add:
Arms: slant-pos.; diagonal pos., forw., sidew.; leaning pos.—Wand and Club ex.—Trunk: bending in obl. directions in stride-pos. forw., sidew.—Legs: lunge in all directions; raise and turn l., r.; swinging in diff. directions, hip-height, bending the other knee; thrusting.—Running in double-quick time.—Skipping forw., backw., sidew.
Breathing ex.: in half-stride pos. forw. on tip-toe, swing arms upw., inhaling.

COMBINATIONS.

Simple and double exercises, simultaneously executed; Double exercises, exec. as consecution of movements; Double exercises, simultaneously executed; Simultaneously exec. exercises of more than two motions.

EIGHTH GRADE—SECOND TERM.

See preceding exercises. Add:
Combinations of preceding order movements in connection with arm, leg ex.—Combinations of all preceding order ex. in running (wheelings, formings, and facings).—Forming in ranks by evasion, forw., backw., sidew.—Forming of the open oblique in front. Same in counter-order. Same in flank.—Forming in ranks of a circle.—Forming of ranks according to the order of forming in ranks.—Combinations, running.—Figure-marching.—Composition.

FREE AND LIGHT GYMNASTICS.

See preceding exercises. Add:
Group ex. with wands—winding.—Support ex.—Antagonistics.—Jumping, running, with leg ex.—Dancing ex. (girls): swaying arms obliquely to one side, cross-stepping. Ex. in double change-step, change hopping triple-step, schottische twirl.—Combination ex.—Hopping and jumping ex. with long ropes (double).—Gymnastic Composition.—The "Reigen."
Breathing ex.: deep breathing.
Plays.

COMBINATIONS.

Double exercises, simultaneously executed; Combination of simultaneously executed exercises.—Variations.—Step ex.—Clubs, (arm and hand circles).—Wands (winding ex.) Dumb-bell exercises.

EIGHTH GRADE—THIRD TERM.

See preceding exercises. Add:
Different methods forming, running on and from place.—Marching sidew. of front or flank ranks in different directions in connection with facings, cross-stepping forw., backw. and alternately (running).—Opening and closing of a column from or towards a given point.—Forming of ranks according to order of forming in ranks.—Forming of ranks in connection with forming in ranks.—Similar and dissimilar forming in bodies and in ranks.

GYMNASIUM EXERCISES.	FIELD EXERCISES.
Exercises in leaning pos. forw., backw., sidew.—Ditto in stooping pos.—Complicated ex. (group ex.) with and without apparatus.—Staccato ex.—Co-operative ex.—Group support ex.—Group ex. with wands and dumb-bells.—Composition. Breathing ex.: inhale, erect pos. rising on tip-toe; exhale, stooping pos. Plays.	Track ex. with hand apparatus.—Class ex. in running, jumping (high, broad, deep, etc.).—Hop, step and jump.—Vaulting ex. (balancing beam, bar).—Throwing, hurling and swinging (grip-balls).—Hurdle running (3' 6").—Throwing the javelin.—Putting the stone.—Pole vaulting. Games: lawn tennis; foot ball; base ball; mount ball.—Discus.

APPARATUS WORK.

(For Games and Plays see C. C. Normal School Series.)

PLAN OF WORK IN THEORY AND PRACTICE OF THE KINDERGARTEN.

Professional Training Class.

FIRST TERM.

The aim of this instruction has been two-fold: First—To give teachers of all grades an insight into Fræbel's kindergarten principles and methods.
Second—To select from these such as are especially adapted to primary work and to enable students to gain some skill in the use of such gifts and occupations as will develop the child's spontaneity, and aid in the all-sided growth of hand, head, heart.
In order to follow a progressive sequence it is necessary that each object presented should contain something of the qualities common to all objects, while at the same time none should be especially emphasized. Every object, therefore, is considered in two ways: (a) As a means by which the child can interpret the external world. (b) A means of self-expression and self-activity.

THE FIRST GIFT.
Six soft worsted balls of prismatic colors.

Leads to the observation and use of elements of

1. Number.
2. Color (transitory and superficial).
3. Material.
4. Movement.
5. Position.
6. Direction.
7. Form (sub-conscious).
8. Songs and games connecting with variously colored fruits, flowers. The "round balls which swing in the air," etc. Wool, sheep and shepherd, etc.

SECOND GIFT. Wooden sphere, cube and cylinder, having same diameter.	Geometry. 1. Conscious differentiation of form. 2. Study of planes, edges (lines) and angles. 3. Associated with various minerals—rock salt, fluorspar, etc., with tree trunks, twigs, parts of human body, etc.

The First and Second Gifts are especially *representative* in their character.

THIRD GIFT. Two-inch wooden cube, divided once in each dimension.	1. Conscious separation into parts. 2. Relation of whole to parts. 3. Construction of new wholes. 4. Law of separation as a fundamental condition for growth observed in seeds, fruits, flowers, etc. 5. Development of social instincts. Development of imagination. N. B.—From first to last the Kindergarten aims to supply the elements for the growth of an imagination which is pure and wholesome. Stories and games presented which illustrate these ideas.
FOURTH GIFT. Two-inch cube, divided once vertically, and three times horizontally.	1. Presents a form especially adapted for *enclosing* space as the preceding gifts had *filled* space. 2. Observation of unequal faces, adaptability for construction, offering elementary lessons in architecture, laying of foundations, building of walls, roofs, arches, etc.
FIFTH AND SIXTH GIFTS. Three-inch cubes variously divided.	Offer enlarged concepts of form, number, relation, etc., and demand increased skill in their manipulation. Connected with various crystalline forms.
SEVENTH GIFT. Small wooden tablets, square and triangular.	Planes studied. Objects represented in two dimensions only.
EIGHTH AND NINTH GIFTS. Sticks and rings.	Objects limited by curves and straight lines. Outlined figures laid and analyzed. Series of figures developed and transformed by additional sticks and rings.

SECOND TERM.

THE OCCUPATIONS.

Parallel with the work with the gifts, there will be sequences of work with more plastic materials by which means the child may freely express, synthetically, those ideas gained through the analysis of preceding objects. The material for these occupations is wholly unsuggestive, until the child's own creative power has been impressed upon it. Thus the clay, cutting and folding paper, painting, weaving, sewing, perforating, all offer a new and permanent embodiment of the ideas of the elementary attributes gained from the preceding objects.

The occupations which will be most used during this term will be the

Folding of squares, circles and triangles to form regular geometric figures.   Cutting and pasting of geometric figures to form sequences of historic ornaments, and

The study of solids and life forms made from cardboard and paper.

THIRD TERM.

Kindergarten games and songs adapted to the sense development, as well as to the development of the social instincts of the children of the Primary School.
Exercises for freedom of movement of entire body.
Exercises in singing.
Exercises in story telling.
Discussion of "music" for children.
Discussion of stories.
Discussion of growth of this Kindergarten Idea.

COURSE OF STUDY IN THEORY AND PRACTICE OF THE KINDERGARTEN - POST GRADUATE.

	SUBJECT.	THEORETICAL AND MECHANICAL WORK WITH THE GIFTS.	SUPPLEMENTARY READING.	OCCUPATIONS.
FIRST TERM.	(1) Anatomy, physiology and hygiene in relation to physiological psychology. Sense perceptions by the infant. Plays with the infant. Their analysis and use. See courses of study in psychology and pedagogics, P. T. class.	First and second gifts.	(1) "First Three Years of Childhood."—Perez. "Outlines in Psychology."—Hoffding. "Opties in Painting."—Helmholtz. "Rhythm in Motion."—Spencer. "Ethics of the Dust."—Ruskin. "Mother Play Book."—Froebel. Chapters in Barnard's Child Culture Papers.	Sewing. Weaving. Paper folding. Black-board drawing. Clay work. Physical culture.
SECOND TERM.	(1) Race History. Relation of the history of the race to the development of the individual. See history of education, P. T. class. (2) History and development of plays and games. (3) Architecture and underlying principles. These principles applied in the simplest constructions. Observations of the application of these same principles in nature.	Third gift. Fourth gift. Fifth gift. Sixth gift. Development of Circle Games.	"Childhood of the World."—Clodd. Old Greek Education.—Mahaffy. The Kindergarten. Susan E. Blow. Stones of Venice.—Ruskin. Special Text-books- Froebel's Education of Man; Miss Peabody's Lectures upon the Kindergarten.	Cutting. Free-weaving. Slat work. Peas work. Physical culture
THIRD TERM.	(1) Stories.. { Myths; their origin. Fairy stories. Realistic stories. (2) Decoration.—Its function in nature and art.	Tablets. Sticks. Rings. Lentils. Making of programs for table work.	"The Use of Stories in the Kindergarten." "Two Paths in Art."—Ruskin. "Talks on Art."—Crane. "Hunt's Talks on Art."—Helen Knowlton.	Modeling. { Clay. { Chalk. Paper intertwining.

SUGGESTIONS FOR FIRST YEAR IN KINDERGARTEN—AGE, 3 TO 4 YEARS.

	Subject.	Number.	Form.	Color.	Direction and Position.	Plays and Games.	Hand Work.
First Term.	1st. To emphasize and lead to the observation by the child, of his personal relations and dependence. Take, for example, his home life, in detail. The life and habits of the animals in relation to himself and to each other. The simplest possible observance of Thanksgiving (the gratitude for the getting of the good things). A simple celebration of Christmas, and the pleasure of giving, emphasized in action.	Groups of 2 and 3. Use of 1 inch, 2 inches, 3 inches by measuring. Countn'n and classification thro' Number. No. in form.	Simple forms in household articles and an attempt made at classification of form. Simple, quick games that will emphasize form and color.	The color of the object or objects at that time, the subject of consideration in the kindergarten.	Front. Back. Up-down. Top-bottom.	The sequence of the gifts preserved in their presentation to the child only, so long as such an order does not interfere with the true expression by the child of the impressions received by him through his observations. The only limitations in the use of the gifts will be his inability to handle the material. The circle game in direct relation to the subject in hand, original with the child, and developed by him under the guidance of the teacher. The simplest possible games that will lead to the development of his senses, and at the same time educate his powers of observation and true expression of his observations in action.	Clay modeling. Sand modeling. Pasting. Sewing.
Second Term.	Food, clothing and shelter—man, animals. Domestic service—in cooking, washing and ironing. Lead out from his home life to his first experience in social life, the kindergarten and surroundings. As each person and thing has a work to perform in the home economy, so in a larger community the same law holds good. Simple weather observations begun.	Same continued. Number used in circle games and marching as a necessity in limitation.	Forms of fruits and vegetables and of domestic utensils. Forms in the kindergarten and their function; as the table, circle, etc., etc.	Same.	Same.		The same continued. Use of scissors in free hand paper cutting of forms in surface then under consideration.
Third Term.	House-cleaning at home—observation of and talking about new things in the home. House cleaning in nature—spring rains. Weather observations continued. His relation with nature. Out-door work in the care of gardens (if possible), and young animals. Work of the spring sun.	Choice by the child of a certain number and judgment by him of the necessity for that particular number.	Forms of tools used in housecleaning, and in the garden, and in the circle plays.	Same	Same.		The same as above. Free painting, paper folding of simple forms at that time being used in the work. Use of garden tools.

*No course of study in the school sense of that term, can be given for a kindergarten.

SUGGESTIONS FOR SECOND YEAR IN KINDERGARTEN—AGE, 4 TO 5 YEARS.

	SUBJECT.	NUMBER.	FORM.	COLOR.	DIRECTION AND POSITION.	PLAYS AND GAMES.	HAND WORK.
FIRST TERM.	Influence of sun and wind in the fall. Observations of nature's preparation for winter in the animal and vegetable kingdoms. Preparation by man. Farmers' stores of food. Thanksgiving celebration, and the dependence and relations of the child broadened. Christmas work, and the "giving" made broader and freer.	Groups of 2, 3 and 4 in table plays, circle games and marching, etc. Single things, lines, form. Judgments of lengths, etc.	Vegetable and animal forms. Forms of trees and leaves. Necessity for forms of farmers' store houses, etc.	Colors in vegetables and fruits. Colors of sunbeams (nature's colors).	Right side. Left side. East. West. Top, bottom. Back, front.	As the child becomes skillful in the use of material, the gifts having the greatest quantity of material may be given him. Demonstration of simple architectural principles.	Clay modeling. Sewing, slat weaving. Paper folding. Paper weaving. Free cutting. Painting.
SECOND TERM.	Frost and its work. Sources of food and clothing. Shelter in homes, schools, etc. Shelter for animals. Observations of weather continued.	Groups of 4 and 5. Analysis of 2, 3, 4 and 5, whenever needed, and synthesis of parts, when possible without forcing.	Snow flakes and ice crystal forms in water, etc. Forms and use of these forms in dwellings and in shelter for animals. Forms of clothing.	How man follows nature in her colors and uses colors on his house, barn, etc.	North. East. West. Right. Left.	The plays and games will increase in their scope for expression by the children in different ways, always appealing directly to their interest and founded on their observation of the subject then in hand.	Blackboard drawing in picturing stories, and objects observed in connection with the above.
THIRD TERM.	Commercial relations and dependence. Carpenter, his work, tools, etc. Gardener, his work, tools, etc. Spring.—Careful observations of trees and animal life. Classification of flowers under color, form and number. Assorting of leaves. Collection of seed.	Groups of 2, 3, 4, 5 and 6, used as above.	Carpenter's and Gardener's tools. Forms of flowers, leaves, plants, trees, etc. Simple architectural forms.	Color of tools and of the flowers, birds, etc.	South. East. West. North. Right. Left.		Work with Carpenter's tools and Gardener's tools. Free painting a special occupation.

SUGGESTIONS FOR THIRD YEAR IN KINDERGARTEN.—AGES 5 TO 6 YEARS.

	SUBJECT.	NUMBER.	FORM.	COLOR.	DIRECTION AND POSITION.	GIFT WORK, CIRCLE GAMES AND HAND-WORK.
FIRST TERM.	Collection and classification of seeds. Calendar kept of fall observations of weather. Influence of weather, of vegetation, animals, etc. The work of the wind. Use made by man of the power of the wind, in mills, transportation, etc., (commercial relations). Work of the miller and farmer. Thanksgiving and Christmas celebrations. Mechanical inventions especially considered.	Groups of 2, 3, 4, 5 and 6. Analysis and synthesis. Judging of dimensions, etc.	Form of seeds, leaves, and classification of each under form.	Fall colors of leaves, seeds, vegetables. Tints and sh'ds in clo'ds, flowers, etc.	Northeast. Southeast. Northwest. Southwest.	The use of the fifth and sixth gifts, in simple architectural forms involving a principle which they work from. Application of these principles in life of plants, animals and man. Use of the principles and forms to intelligently construct necessary articles in common use.
SECOND TERM.	Manufacture of woolen or cotton goods, in mills. Where we buy our clothes to keep us warm. Dealers in dry goods. Winter weather, frost and snow. What keeps our house warm. Fire and its use in homes, in factories, transportation, etc. Use of water with fire in these factories.	Differ't stories in mills, and use. Val'u's of things bought. Plays involving the buying and selling of articles.	Form in machinery and in fire places, boilers, etc., and form in its use generally in inventions.	Tints and sh'd's in clothing. Colors in the fire.	Groupings of buildings for convenience, having direction and position clearly emphasized.	The circle games, always carrying out in action and design the leading thought, and being suggested and worked out by the children.
THIRD TERM.	Use of water in homes and in manufactories. Rain and its work in nature with regard to vegetation, structure, etc. Gardening.	Same continued. Number in nurobing.	Rain drops. Streams. Young leaves. General outline of trees, etc.	Flowers, grass, sh'd's of earth when dry or wet, or different in color from other causes.	Direction of wind and rain and the relative position of stream and pond, etc.	The hand-work, increasing in complexity with added skill, but always carrying out the leading thought of the gift-work and giving scope for the inventive power of the child.

SPECIAL TEACHERS.

Each special teacher has full charge and supervision of a subject of study or art, both in the Training Class and the Practice School. The duties are: (1) to teach the subject in the Training Class in order to prepare its members for practice teaching; (2) to carefully examine all plans of teaching and approve or disapprove of them; (3) to thoroughly supervise the practice teaching; (4) to teach the psychology and methods pertaining to the subject which he or she teaches; (5) to teach, advise and criticise the critic teachers and the work of the Practice School; (6) to take a full share in the order and government of the school; (7) to attend all teachers' meetings; (8) to prepare courses of study and manuals in the subjects under his supervision.

CRITIC TEACHERS.

Each critic teacher has charge of a grade or room in the Practice School, her duties are: (1) to teach and train the pupils in her room; (2) to have full supervision of the pupil-teachers while teaching groups of her grade; (3) to assign positions to pupil-teachers, to choose group leaders, section and division leaders and recommend assistant teachers; (4) to assign subjects for plans of teaching and approve or disapprove of them; (5) to see that no pupil is assigned the same subject twice until she has taught all the subjects; (6) to thoroughly supervise the practice teaching during the practice hour; (7) to criticise personally each pupil-teacher under her supervision; (8) to assist in the order and government of the whole school; (9) to attend all the teachers' meetings.

TEACHERS' MEETINGS.

The regular Faculty Meeting occurs every Monday evening, 7:30 to 9:15, at the house of the Principal. In this and other meetings all the work of the school is thoroughly discussed.

RULES AND DIRECTIONS FOR THE PROFESSIONAL TRAINING CLASS.

1. Upon entering the class, show your diplomas, certificates and other credentials to the vice-principal, who will give you a blank to be carefully filled out.
2. You will then be assigned to a grade for practice-teaching and also appointed as a member of one of the working committees.
3. From the chairman and other members of the working committee you will get full information in regard to your duties in the school.
4. The one rule of the school is: "Everything to help and nothing to hinder." You are recognized as a *teacher* with all the duties and responsibilities of a teacher. The "housekeeping" of the school, the care of rooms, books, apparatus and material, forms a main feature in the training of teachers.
5. You are expected to be prompt, punctual, always in your place when possible, always ready for work; in fact, you are expected to realize your ideal of a teacher in your work and conduct.
6. Please never leave the school or be absent from a class or exercise without a proper excuse.
7. You are expected to do no more than is possible for you to do and keep in an excellent state of health.
8. Each month you will carefully prepare a plan for teaching; this plan must be approved by the critic-teacher in your grade and by the special-teacher before you are allowed to teach.
9. Please apply for criticism to the teachers who have taught you or observed your work.
10. The standpoints of personal criticism may be stated as follows; (a) effort to work, (b) direction of work, is it economical? (c) economy of time, (d) courage and persistence in overcoming difficulties, (e) love manifested for work, (f) motive of work, (g) skill in modes of expression, (h) practice teaching, (i) helpfulness, housekeeping, trustworthiness, (j) progress, (k) influence, (l) quality of work.
11. The purpose of the three divisions of the Professional Training Class is to put each student into a community where he or she will do the most good. According to the standpoints of criticism a member of the third division may far excel in effort anyone in the first division.

RULES FOR THE LIBRARY.

The reference books must not be taken from the library, but freely used by the pupils for reference during work hours.
The other books may be drawn on the regular library slips for such periods as the librarian may stipulate.
Books singly or in sets may be drawn by the regular grade teacher for room work.
TEACHERS ARE MADE RESPONSIBLE FOR THE BOOKS DRAWN BY THEM.
Members of the P. T. Class are also held responsible for books drawn on their name.
Children's books may be drawn by the grade pupils on library cards (5 cents each) for a period of one week, with the privilege of renewal for a second week.

RULES FOR STUDENTS' HALL.

Breakfast from .... 7.00—8.00 A. M.
Luncheon from.. 12.30—1.15 P. M.
Dinner from... 6.00—7.00 P. M.
Study Hours... 7.15—9.30 P. M.
Office Hours of Manager.............................. { 8.00—9.00 A. M.
                                                                    { 4.00—6.00 P. M.

1. Be in dining-room promptly after ringing of the bell. No meals served after regular hours. Meals taken to rooms will be charged extra.

2. Board must be paid in advance to the manager on the first Monday of each month. No reduction will be made for any fraction of a week. By giving notice, when the house is not crowded, the friends of students will be entertained at the rate of $1.00 per day.

3. Anyone burning gas after 10.30 P. M. will be charged 25 cents per week extra. Students leaving their rooms, whether for a long or short time, must extinguish the gas.

4. The laundry will be open for use of students from 5.30 A. M. to 5.30 P. M. on Saturdays. Clothes for washing will not be received after 9.00 A. M., Tuesday. Visiting the kitchen will not be permitted and all familiarity with servants must be avoided.

5. All waste paper, etc., must be deposited in the waste basket in the corridors. Do not throw anything out of the windows. Combings, banana peelings, etc., must not be thrown in slop buckets or the water closets.

6. Slop buckets must not be left in bath-rooms or halls. The washing of handkerchiefs or articles of clothing in the bath rooms is absolutely forbidden.

7. Students must study in their own rooms during study hours. After 7.15 absolute quiet must be observed both in halls and rooms.

8. All complaints in regard to food, service, room or upon any subject whatever, must be made directly to the manager during regular office hours and no other time. If the matter is not satisfactorily adjusted by the manager, the complaint may be made to the principal. Any gossip or discussion in regard to complaints is strictly forbidden.

9. Each occupant of a room is responsible for its condition, and any damage to furniture or carpets must be at once reported to the manager and paid for.

10. One general rule is sufficient for the members of Students' Hall. Every one is expected to be a lady or gentleman in deportment and character; for any deviation from this rule, anyone forfeits his or her right to remain in Students' Hall or in the school.

11. Young ladies who expect to go out for the evening must leave their names with the manager, and state where and with whom they are going, and at what hour they will return.

12. Students' Hall is for (1st) residents of the county who are members of the school (2d) For other members of the school. (3d) If the rooms are not all taken by members of the school, the manager may take others, with the understanding that they must give up their rooms if needed for students. Board for ladies, $3.50 per week; for gentlemen, $4.00 per week.   Mrs. Florence J. Gardiner, Manager.
                                                        Approved:
                                                          Francis W. Parker, Principal.

RULES FOR HEATING AND VENTILATION.

1. The engineer will make a tour of the building at 8.30 A. M. and attend to all of the registers. He will also make a second tour at 11.00 A. M. and a third at 2.00 P. M.

2. The officer of the day will have general supervision over the heating and ventilation in the entire building.

3. Each lieutenant will have immediate supervision of the heating and ventilation on the floor to which he or she is assigned.

4. The ventilation is effected by means of cold air ducts; the registers entering these are in the sides of the rooms. *These must always be kept open.* When the ventilation is not sufficient by these means, open the windows a *very little* at the top.

5. The heating is effected by means of hot air through registers in the floors and walls of the rooms and halls. If the temperature reaches 75° the registers are to be closed until 68° is reached and then they may be opened. If the temperature of any room falls below 65° when the hot air registers are open, the lieutenants must notify the engineer and specify the room.

6. The engineer will make visits to the Boarding Hall at 9.00 and 11.00 A. M., and at 2.30 and 5.00 P. M. Information regarding the temperature of the hall will be posted at the foot of the stairs, east end of the building.

7. ALL TEACHERS ARE RESPECTFULLY REQUESTED TO BE VERY CAREFUL ABOUT THE HEATING AND VENTILATION.

ITEMS OF INFORMATION.

It is proposed in these "Items" to answer the questions often asked in letters addressed to the Principal.

Term — The year (forty weeks) is divided into three terms, as follows: The Fall Term begins on the first Monday in September, and continues sixteen weeks.

The Winter Term begins the first Monday after New Year's, and continues twelve weeks.

The Spring Term begins the first Monday after April 1st, and continues twelve weeks.

Standard of Admission. — Graduates of colleges, universities, other regular Normal Schools, graduates of accredited high schools, full four years' course, teachers of three years' successful experience, who hold first-grade certificates, are admitted *at any time* to the Professional Training Class, on presentation of the proper diplomas and other credentials.

Curriculum of the Professional Training Class. — The work of the Training Class is strictly professional; it is adapted to students and teachers of whatever grade, education or experience. The lines of progress are so arranged that each student can do his best in independent work in any direction.

There is no high school or academic work done in the school.

Subjects of Study. — The professional subjects of study are psychology, pedagogics, history of education, methods of teaching and the theory of the Kindergarten.

Preparation for Practice Teaching. — In direct preparation for practice teaching, the sciences, geography, history, literature and mathematics (number and arithmetic, form and geometry), are thoroughly reviewed.

Preparation for Thought Expression. — The class have continual practice and training, in gesture, elocution, vocal music, modeling (in sand, clay and putty, and chalk modeling in geography), painting, drawing, speech, writing and physical culture throughout the course.

Graduates, Students and Teachers who wish to Study Before Entering the School. — Students and teachers who wish to specially prepare for professional study before entering the school are referred to the manuals prepared for the Training Class: "How to Study Geography," "Nature Study," "Outlines of History," "Suggestions and Directions for Teaching Language," and "Exercises in Elocution."

Time for Graduation. — No student is allowed to graduate until he or she has been a member of the Training Class for one year or forty weeks; this time need not be continuous. Students are strongly advised to remain in the Professional Training Class at least two years.

Standard for Graduation. — The standard for graduation is the ability to teach and govern a school in Cook County.

Elective or Post-Graduate Courses. — Students are not permitted to take elective or post-graduate courses until they have received diplomas of graduation. The Kindergarten Training Class is a post-graduate course.

Teachers' Certificates. — Each graduate receives at time of graduation a teacher's certificate, valid for Cook County outside of the city of Chicago.

The County Superintendent of Schools grants two grades of certificates, first and second. The second grade certificate is given to all graduates. First grade certificates will be issued to graduates as soon as they have shown *marked ability* in teaching and managing schools in Cook County.

Teachers' Positions for Graduates. Although no promises of position are ever made to students, all graduates have hitherto readily found good positions in Cook County or elsewhere.

No Pledge to teach in the County Required. No pledge to teach in Cook County is required of students, the graduates, however, with very few exceptions do teach in the county and city.

The Professional Training Class is free to *bona-fide* residents of Cook County, including the city of Chicago.

Expenses. Tuition Fee. Non-residents. Non-residents pay seventy-five dollars ($75.00) tuition per year. The tuition is payable in advance at the beginning of each term: $30.00 for Fall Term, and $22.50 for Winter and Spring Terms respectively. Miss Mary M. Weaver, treasurer, receives the tuition—office in library. The same tuition is required for all post-graduate courses including the Kindergarten.

Library. The money received for tuition is used to buy books for the library and for the purchase of apparatus.

Cost of one year. The cost of one year's membership of the Professional Training Class to non-residents, may be estimated as follows:

FOR WOMEN.

Board $3.50 per week, forty weeks	$140 00
Tuition	75 00
Estimated cost of books, stationery and other necessary incidentals	30 00
Total	$245 00

FOR MEN.

Board $4.00 per week, forty weeks	$160 00
Tuition	75 00
Estimated cost of books, stationery and other necessary incidentals	30 00
Total	$265 00

Students Hall. Students' Hall is a boarding house provided by the county for the school. The price of board, including room, heating and lighting, is $3.50 per week for ladies, $4.00 per week for gentlemen. The lady students are expected to furnish sheets, pillow-cases, towels, napkins and white bed spread.

The Manager. All inquiries concerning board, and all requests and orders, must be sent to Mrs. Florence J. Gardiner, Manager Students' Hall, Englewood, Ill.

Persons who intend to board at the hall are requested to inform the Manager in advance.

Institutes. The Superintendent of Schools, Cook County, holds a Teachers' Institute at the Normal School, during the week preceding the opening of the school in September. The entire faculty teach in this institute.

This Institute is free to all persons holding a teacher's certificate in force in Cook County outside of Chicago; other persons pay a tuition of $1.00.

September Institute. During the month of September an Institute is held in connection with the Training Class, for teachers whose schools begin later than September

1st. This Institute is free to all persons holding Cook County teachers' certificates, and other persons, residents of the county, who are eligible to the Training Class. Non-residents pay a tuition of $7.50 per month.

Practice School. Boundaries of Sub-districts. The Practice School is a regular public school of the city of Chicago. The Practice School sub-district lies between the middle of 65th St. on the north and the middle of 75th St. on the south; and between the Rock Island and Eastern Illinois on the east and west. All pupils within these boundaries are admitted to the Practice School free of tuition.

Admission by Transfer. Whenever there is room in the Practice School, the City Superintendent of Schools (office on 3d floor of City Hall) will grant transfers to the Normal School on personal application.

Location of School. The Cook County Normal School is on 68th St. and Stewart Ave., seven and one-half miles due south of the Palmer House. Normal Park is in the southern part of Englewood.

The stations of the Eastern Illinois and Rock Island railroads are in Normal Park close to the school.

The Erie, Monon, Wabash, Chicago & Evansville, stop at station on 63d St., Englewood, five blocks north and three and one-half blocks west of the school. The Rock Island, except some through trains, stop at Normal Park; all trains on this road stop at 62d St., Englewood. The Lake Shore trains also stop at 62d St; the Pittsburgh & Ft. Wayne at 63d St.

Upon arriving over other roads, persons must first go to a main station in the city, and then come to Normal Park upon the Eastern Illinois, Rock Island or cable. By taking the State street cable and transferring at the viaduct to the Auburn Park car, one can stop at 68th St., near the school.

All railroads sell commutation tickets on suburban trains. The Eastern Illinois sells ten-trip tickets for 60 cts., and the Rock Island the same for $1.10.

Check baggage to Normal Park or Englewood, if possible.

TEXT-BOOKS AND LIBRARY.

The Library contains 12,000 volumes of very carefully selected books for study. The books are for the free use of the pupils and teachers.

TEXT-BOOKS FOR TRAINING CLASS.

Members of the Training Class and Practice School are requested to purchase books as designated below:

TRAINING CLASS.

SCIENCE.

"Nature Study," a guide to the study and teaching of science.
"Colton's Zoology;" any good manual for dissecting will answer.
"Crosby's Tables," for the determination of minerals.
"Gray's Field, Forest and Garden Botany."
"Science Record Book for Daily Observation."
Set of Dissecting Instruments.

HISTORY.

"Outlines of History."

GEOGRAPHY.

"How to Study Geography."

PRACTICE SCHOOL.

FIRST GRADE.

"Harper's First Reader."

SECOND GRADE.

"Harper's Second Reader."

THIRD GRADE.

"Stickney's Third Reader."
"Robinson's Beginners' Arithmetic."

FOURTH GRADE.

"Harper's Third Reader."
"Robinson's Beginners' Arithmetic."
Dictionary (High School).
"Science Record."

FIFTH GRADE.

"Robinson's Beginners' Arithmetic."
Dictionary (High School).
"Science Record"
"Sheldon's American History."

SIXTH GRADE.

"Robinson's Arithmetic."
"Butler's Geography."
"Sheldon's American History."
Dictionary (High School).
"Science Record."

SEVENTH GRADE.

"Science Record."
"Butler's Geography."
"Robinson's Graded Lessons in Arithmetic."
"Fiske's American History."
Dictionary (High School).

EIGHTH GRADE.

"Butler's Geography."
"Robinson's Graded Lessons in Arithmetic."
"Fiske's History of the United States."
"Meikeljohn's English Language."
Dictionary (High School).
"Science Record."

www.ingramcontent.com/pod-product-compliance
Lightning Source LLC
Chambersburg PA
CBHW031410160426
43196CB00007B/967